BABY NAMES
for AFRICAN CHILDREN

Tyra Mason & Sam Chekwas

SEABURN

New York

ISBN: 1-885778-35-X

Cover design by Cheryl Hanna
Cover concept by Sam Chekwas
All rights reserved

Seaburn Publishing
PO Box 2085
Long Island City, New York 11102
Tel. (718) 274-1300

MANUFACTURED IN THE UNITED STATES

WHAT IS IN A NAME

The naming ceremony is a momentous tradition throughout the African continent. It is told that when Elekwa was born, his father was away on a fishing expedition struggling in the high seas with the winds and dark forces of the ocean. His new born son, noting his absence was in constant search for his father. The agitated child was named Elekwa for looking around, wondering and crying. When his father finally returned from the expedition, the first question he asked was "where is Elekwa", because he was spiritually in contact with his son.

We are disappointed by the names that people claim to be Ibo, Yoruba or categorized as African. The demand for baby name books is booming so companies contract people who have no knowledge of African names, to compile name books with so called African origin. In a popular name book for African American children, the name Chijioke: God gives wisdom, is translated as a Yoruba name for power money; Ikechukwu, a popular Ibo name is translated as a Yoruba name for God of fire; Ifeachu, is translated as Yoruba for God's child and Ezebueni is translated as a Yoruba name for love. All of these meanings are wrong.

Let us give our children some identity and pride, starting with their names. Let us name our children Hubert: German for bright, shining mind, rather than Houston: Scottish for name of a town.

When a child is named Akweke: Ibo for the egg of a boa, let it be known that the child is valuable, delicate and precious.

GIVE OUR CHILDREN PRIDE, GIVE THEM NAMES WITH VALUABLE MEANINGS.

NICKNAMES AND PARACHUCKLES

In Africa name calling is a common phenomenon. On many occasions, a visitor finds it hard to distinguish what the real name of an individual is, since almost everyone in the community has a special name or nick name (usually positive) that they allocate to friends, family, strangers or even to their enemies.

My mother usually called me Agu: Lion, often when I performed difficult labor; Oje-alo: One who goes and shall return; when I run errands successfully...

Most of this name calling in many cases take a turn for the bizarre. My grandfather was often called - Ori-isi-Agu: One who eats the head of a lion, and I have always wondered if he actually performed that feat.

MY FAVORITE NAMES FOR MY WIFE: REAL NAME: Tyra

Enyi di ya: Friend of her husband; Nnennem: My mothers mother; Ada-ukwu: My big daughter, and of course my all-time favorite: Ty Bebe-Gugginheimer; for the mother of my daughter (Guggin) and Tiger; when she accomplishes a task.

FOR MY DAUGHTER: REAL NAME: Chinyere Zoe

Guggin; often when I want to tickle her; Chichi, Chi Bebe; Chakpina; when she is restless; Ada-oma: beautiful daughter; Enyinnaya: Her father's best friend; Enyioma: beautiful friend, Ada-ukwu, Kisisibebe, and more.

FOR MY SISTER: REAL NAME: Chidinma

Chichi nwa Beke: Chichi the white woman - refering to her light complexion and graceful demeanor. Nwanyioma: beautiful lady. Adaokporoko: daughter of stockfish - refering to her legendary cooking with the delicious stockfish. Ori-aku diya: one who enjoys the wealth of her husband.

Most nicknames and parachuckles reflect the character and demeanor of the individuals to whom the names are given and often help shape their personalities too. Friends who do not carve out names for one another are considered temporary or superficial friends.

What name do you have for your loved ones, ENYIM-O !

Dedicated to all our children and to our love

Contents

TRIBES OF AFRICA

Agikuyu	Bulala	Ga
Akamba	Calabar	Gabbra
Akan	Chewa	Gbaya
Asante	Dogon	Hausa
Azande	Elmolo	Herero
Bagirmi	Ewe	Hindi
Banda	Ewe	Ibo or Igbo
Batswana	Fang	Khoi
Bemba	Fante	Kipsigis
Benin	Fulani	Kongo
Bini		Kuba
Booran		

LANGUAGES OF AFRICA

Lozi	Mossi	Songhai
Luba	Ndali	Soninke
Luo	Ndali	Swahili
Maasai	Ndebele	Swahili
Makonde	Ngoni	Swazi
Malinke	Ngori	Teda
Mangbetu	Nyakyusa	Tswana
Mbundu	Ogidi	Turkana
Mbuti	Pokot	Wolof
Mende	Rendille	Xhosa
Mende	Samburu	Yao
Mijikenda	Shona	Yoruba
Mongo	Shona	Yoruba
		Yoruba
		Zulu

AFRICAN LEADERS

ALGERIA
Ahmed Ben Bella
Houari Boumedienne
Chadli Bendjedid
Mohamed Boudiaf

ANGOLA
Agostinho Neto
Jose' Eduardo dos Santos

BENIN
Hubert Maga
Sourou-Migan Apithy
Christophe Soglo
Emile-Derlin Zinsou
Justin Ahomadegba
Apithy Maga
Mathieu Karekou
Nicephore Soglo

BOTSWANA
Seretse M. Khama
Quett K.J.Masire

BURKINO FASO
Maurice Yameogo
Sangoule' Lamizana
Saye' Zerbo
Jean-Baptiste Oudraogo
Thomas Sankara
Blaise Compaore

BURUNDI
Mwami Mwambutsa IV
Mwami (King) Natare V
Michel Micombero
Jean-Baptiste Bagaza
Pierre Buyoya

CAMEROON
Ahmadou B. Ahidjo
Paul Biya

CAPE VERDE
Aristides Maria Pereira
Antonio Mandiarsarai

CA REPUBLIC
David Dacko
Jean-Bedel Bokassa
Andre D. Kolingba

CHAD
Francois Tombalbaye
Felix Malloum
Goukhouni Oueddei
Hissein Habre
Idriss Deby

COMOROS
Prince Jaffar
Ahmed A. Abderrmane
Ali Soilih
Said Mohamed Djohar

CONGO
Fulbert Youlou
Alphonse Massamba-Debat
Marien Ngouabi
Joachim Yhombi-Opango
Denis Sassou-Nguesso
Andre Milongo

COTE D'IVOIRE
Felix Houphouet-Boigny

DJIBOUTI
Hassan Gouled Aptidon

EGYPT
Muhannad Nagib
Gamal Adbel Nasser
Muhammad Anwar-Sadat
Muhammad Hosni Mubarak

EQUATORIAL GUINEA
Macie Nguema Biyogo
Negue Ndong
Tedoro O. Nguema Mbasogo

ETHIOPIA
Haile Mariam Selassie I
Mengistu Haile-Miriam

Meles Zenawi

GABO
Leon M'Ba
El Hadj Omar Bongo

GAMBIA
Alhaji D. Kairaba Jawara

GHANA
Kwame N. Nkrumnah
Joseph A. Ankrah
Kofi A Busia
Ignatius K. Acheampong
Frederick W.F. Akuffo
Hilla Limann
Jerry John Rawlings

GUINEA
Ahmed Sekou Toure
Lansana Beavogui
Lansana Conte

GUINEA-BISSAU
Luis De Almeida Cabral
Jao Bernardo Vieira

KENYA
Jomo Kenyatta
Daniel Teroitich arap Moi

LESOTHO
King Moshoeshoe II
King Letsie III

LIBERIA
Garrett W. Gibson
Arthur Barclay
Daniel E. Howard
Charles D.B. King
Edwin Barclay
William V.S. Tubman
William Richard Tolbert, Jr.
Samuel K. Doe
Amos Sawyer

LIBYA
Muhammad al-Sanussi
Mu'ammar A. Qadhafi

MADAGASCAR
Philibert Tsiranana
Richard Ratsimandrava
Gabriel Ramanantsoa
Didier Ratsiraka

MALAWI
Ngwazi H. Kamuzu Banda

MALI
Modibo Keita
Moussa Traore
Amadou Toumani Toure
Alpha Oumar Konare

MAURITANIA
Mokar Ould Daddah
Mustapha Ould Selek
Mohamed Mahmoud Ould
Ahmed Louly
Mohamed K. Haidalla
Maaouya O.S. Ahmed Taya

MAURITIUS
Seewoosagur Ramgoolam
Aneerood Jugnauth

MOROCCO
King Mohamed V
King Hassan II

MOZAMBIQUE
Samora Machel
Joaquim Alberto Chissano

NAMIBIA
Sam Shafilshuna Nujoma

NIGER
Hamani Diori
Seyni Kountche
Ali Saibou

NIGERIA
Nnamdi Azikiwe
Johnson Aguiyi-Ironsi
Yakubu Gowon
Murtala Ramat Muhammad
Olusegun Obasanjo
Shehu Shagari

RWANDA
Gregoire Kayibanda
Juvenal Habyarimana

SAO TOME PRINCIPE
Manuel Pinto de Costa
Miguel Anjos de Cunha
Liisboa Travoada

SENEGAL
Leopold Sedar Senghor
Abdou Diouf

SEYCHELLES
James Richard Manchum
France Albert Rene

SIERRA LEONE
Milton Margai
Albrt M. Margai
Andrew Juxon-Smith
Siaka Probyn Stevens
Joseph Saidu Momoh

SOMALIA
Abdirashid Ali Shermarke
Mohamed Siad Barre
Ali Mahdi Mohamed

SOUTH AFRICA
Hendrik F. Verwoerd
Balthazar J. Vorster
Pieter Willem Botha
Frederik Willem Deklerk
Nelson Mandela

SUDAN
Ibrahim Abbud
Muhammad A. Mahgub
Ja'far Muhammad Numayri

Abdel Rahman al-Dahab
Sadiq al-Mahdi
Umar Hassan al-Bashir

SWAZILAND
King Sobhuza II
Queen Ntombi Thwala
King Mswati III

TANZANIA
Julius Kambarage Nyerere
Ali Hassan Mwinyi

TOGO
Sylvanus Olympio
Nicolas Grunitzky
Gnassingbe Eyadema

TUNISIA
Habib Bourguiba
Zine El-Abidine Ben Ali

UGANDA
Kabbaka Yekka
Milton Obote
Idi Amin Dada
Useful Lule
Godfrey Binaisa
Tito Okello Lutwa
Yoweri Kaguta Musevini

ZAIRE
Patrice Lumumba
Moise Tshombe
Mobutu Sese Seko Kuku

ZAMBIA
Kenneth David Kaunda

ZIMBABWE
Canaan Sodindo Banana
Robert Gabriel Mugabe

A name is like the palm oil which yam is consumed

Ibo saying

A

Aanuolu   Yoruba: Mercy of God
Aarinola   Yoruba: Centre of honor
Aaron   Biblical: Enlightened, lofty
Aba   WA: Born on Thursday
Abaecheta   Ibo: When one gets wealthy one is remembered
Abam   Akan: Next child
Abanobi   WA: There's no entrance to the mind
Abasi   NA: Prophet of Muhammad's uncle
Abasi   WA: Stern
Abayaa   Akan: Born on Yawda (Thursday)
Abayomi   Yoruba: She brings joy
Abdalla   NA: Servant of God
Abdu   NA: Servant God
Abdul   NA: Servant of the lord
Abdul-rahman   NA: Servent of God
Abdulaziz   NA: Servant of the dear one
Abdulbasit   NA: Servant of the extender
Abdulfhaliq   NA: Servant of the creator
Abdulghaffaar   NA: Servant of the forgiver
Abdulghaffuur   NA: Servant of the forgiving
Abdulghani   NA: Servant of the prosperous
Abdulhaliim   NA: Servant of the clement
Abdulhamid   NA: Servant of the praiseworthy
Abduljabbaar   NA: Servant of the brave one
Abduljamiil   NA: Servant of the majestic
Abdulkarim   NA: Servant of the bountiful
Abdulla   NA: Servant of God
Abdullah   NA: Servant of God
Abdullahi   NA: Servant of God

Abdullatif   Arabic: Servant of the kind one
Abdulmajiid   NA: Servant of the glorious
Abdulmalik   NA: Servant of the king
Abdulmuti   NA: Servant of the doner
Abdulnassar   NA: Servant of the savior
Abdulqaadir   NA: Servant of the able
Abdulqudduus   NA: Servant of the most Holy
Abdulrazzaaq   NA: Servant of the provider
Abdulwaahab   NA: Servant of the bestower
Abdulwaahid   NA: Servant of the one; Abdulwahiid
Abdulwakiil   NA: Servant of the trustee
Abdurrahim   NA: Servant of the merciful
Abdurrahman   NA: Servant of the beneficient
Abdurrasul   NA: Servant of the messenger
Abdurrauf   NA: Servant of the compassionate
Abdussamed   NA: Servant of the eternal
Abebi   Yoruba: Delivered
Abebja   WA: Born at a time of grief
Abedi   NA: Worshipper
Abeeku   WA: Born on Wednesday
Abegunde   Yoruba: Born during the Egungun festival
Abeid   EA: He is a leader
Abeje   Yoruba: We asked to have her
Abeke Yoruba: To be loved
Abel   Biblical: The second son of Adam and Eve
Abena   WA: Born on Tuesday
Abeni   Yoruba: Behold she is ours
Abeo   Yoruba: Born with wealth
Abi   WA: To guard
Abia   WA: Shall return
Abiade   WA: Born of royal parents
Abiba   NA: The beloved one
Abidemi   Shekiri: Refined
Abifarin   Yoruba: One who walks in Ifa
Abike   Yoruba: One born to be petted
Abimbola   Yoruba: Born to be rich
Abiodum   Yoruba: One born during a festival
Abiola   Yoruba: Born in honor
Abiona   Yoruba: One who is born on the roadside
Abiose   Yoruba: One born on the Sabbath

Abioye   Yoruba: One who is born into a chieftaincy title
Abir   Arabic: Fragrant
Abisogun   Yoruba: One born during a war
Abla   Swahili: A wild rose
Ablah   Arabic: Perfectly
Aboaronye   WA: Whom are you threatening?
Aboderin   Yoruba: One who walks with a hunter
Abodunrin   Yoruba: One who walks in at a festival
Aborisade   Yoruba: One who arrives with the orisa
Abosede   Yoruba: One who arrives on the day Sabbath
Abosi   WA: Life plant
Aboyade   Yoruba: One who returns with the Oya river
Abraham   Biblical: Father of a mighty nation, blessed by God
Abu   WA: Nobility
Abubakar   NA: The first Khalifa after Prophet Muhammad
Abubakar   WA: Noble
Abubaker   Successor after the death of Prophet Muhammad
Abubudike   Ibo: Man of prowess
Abuchi   Ibo: Nobody is god to the other
Abudu   Swahili: NA: Aboud servant of God
Abuu   NA: Father
Abwooli   Uganda: Cat
Achama   Ibo: One that is light skined is beautiful
Achionye   Ibo: Who is being governed
Acholam   Ibo: Do not provoke me
Achufusi   WA: Do not reject
Ada   WA: First daughter
Adabuaku   Ibo: A daughter that would bring wealth
Adachi   Ibo: The daughter of god
Adaego   WA: Daughter of wealth
Adaeke   WA: Born on Eke market day
Adaeze   Ibo: Princess
Adam   Biblical: First human being
Adama   WA: Majestic
Adamu   NA: Adam the first human being
Adan   NA: Good fortune
Adande   WA: The challenger
Adanma   WA: Daughter of beauty
Adanna   Ibo: Daughter of her father; Adannaya
Adanne   Ibo: Daughter of her mother

Adanta   Ibo: The younger daughter
Adaoha   Ibo: Daughter of the people
Adaoma   Ibo: Adanma, Adamma Beautiful daughter
Adaramaja   Yoruba: One who does not quarrel
Adaramola   Yoruba: Good natured
Adaugo   Ibo: Daughter of an eagle, A daughter of high esteem
Adaukwu   Ibo: Senior daughter, Big sister
Addae   WA: Morning sun
Ade   WA: Crown
Adeagbo   Yoruba: Crown of the family
Adebayo   WA: He came in a joyful time
Adebiyi   Yoruba: Crown gave birth to this
Adebomi   WA: Crown had covered my nakedness
Adebomi   Yoruba: The crown covers my nakedness
Adebusuyi   Yoruba: The crown adds to diginity
Aded   WA: The crown is shattered
Adedagbo   WA: Happiness is crown
Adedapo   Yoruba: Crowns are mixed together
Adedeji   Yoruba: Crowns become two
Adediran   Yoruba: Crowns become hereditary
Adedoja   Yoruba: Crown becomes a market
Adedotum   Yoruba: Crown becomes anew
Adedoyin   Yoruba: Crown becomes honey
Adefarasin   Yoruba: The crown is hidden away
Adefolake   Yoruba: The crown favors him
Adefolarin   Yoruba: The crown walked with honor
Adefoluke   Yoruba: The crown cared for this child with the help of God
Adegbite   Yoruba: Crown receives praises from neighboring clans
Adegbola   Yoruba: Crown receives honor
Adeiye   Yoruba: Crown of salvation
Adekemi   Yoruba: Crown takes care of me
Adekogbe   Yoruba: The crown refuses the bush
Adekola   Yoruba: Crown demands honor
Adelabu   Yoruba: Crown crosses deep waters
Adelaja   WA: A crown is added to my wealth
Adelana   Yoruba: Crown cuts a path
Adelanwa   Yoruba: It is a crown
Adelanwa   Yoruba: It's a crown we are looking for
Adeleke   Yoruba: The crown triumphs
Adeleke   Yoruba: The crown brings happiness

Adeloye   Yoruba: Essence of the crown
Adelugba   Yoruba: The crown is his
Adeniji   Yoruba: Crown offers protection
Adenike   Yoruba: Crown has obligation to care
Adeniyi   Yoruba: Crown has dignity
Adenrele   Yoruba: The crown is going home
Adenuga   Yoruba: The crown has a palace
Adeola   WA: Crown brings honor
Adeola   Yoruba: Crown of high estates
Adeosun   Yoruba: Crown of Osun
Adeoye   Yoruba: Crown of a title
Adepoju   Yoruba: Plentiful
Aderinola   Yoruba: Crowned
Adero   CA: She gives life
Adesanya   Yoruba: The crown compensates for suffering
Adesigbin   Yoruba: Obatala's drum
Adesola   Yoruba: Crown makes a fanfare
Adesoye   Yoruba: Crown watches over a title
Adetero   Yoruba: The crown is in order
Adetola   Yoruba: A crown is enough to boast about
Adetowun   Yoruba: Crown is enough to elate one
Adetutu   Yoruba: Crown is comfortable
Adeyefa   Yoruba: The crown Ifa
Adeyemi   Yoruba: Crown befits me
Adeyemo   Yoruba: A crown befits the child
Adeyinka   Yoruba: Crown surrounds me
Adhra   Swahili: Apology
Adia   Swahili: A gift from God has come
Adiagha   WA: First daughter
Adiba   Arabic: She is born in want of parents
Adiele   Ibo: One is watching to see
Adiezemma   Ibo: The kings favorite
Adika   WA: First child of a second husband
Adike   Ibo: Is one strong enough?
Adil   NA: ('adil) Just
Adila   Swahili: Fair
Adila   Swahili: Just upright
Adimma   Ibo: Is one good?
Adisa   WA: One who makes himself clear
Adiva   Arabic: Gentle

Adjua   WA: Noble
Adla   Swahili: Justice
Adoa   Akan: Born Saturday
Adocha   Ibo: Fair complexioned daughter
Adong   EA: No father was present
Adonis   Greek: A handsome lord
Adrian   Latin: Black or dark one
Adubiifa   Yoruba: One who is black like Ifa
Aduke   WA: Much loved
Aduke   Yoruba: Plentiful
Adun   Shekiri: I struggle
Adunni   Yoruba: Sweet
Adwin   WA: Artist
Adwiukwu   Ibo: Is one great?
Adwoa   Akan: Born on Monday
Adzo   WA: Born on Monday
Afaafa   Swahili: Virtue
Afafa   Ghana: First child of second husband
Afam   WA: Friendly
Afi   WA: Born on Friday
Afi   Ghana: Spritual
Afiba   WA: By the sea
Afifa   Swahili: Virtuous
Afiya   Swahili: Health
Afolabi   Yoruba: A child born with high status
Afolayan   Yoruba: One who struts around with fame
Afoma   Ibo: Good womb that produces good children
Afonne   Ibo: Mother's womb
Afra   Arabic: White
Afrika   Swahili: Africa
Afryea   WA: Born during happy times
Afua   Ghana: Born on Friday
Afua   Swahili: Forgiveness
Agbaje   Yoruba: One who carries prosperity on the throne
Agbaraoji   Ibo: The spirit of the iroko tree
Agbaraoke   Ibo: Prime spirit
Agbeke   Yoruba: One to be carried and petted
Agbeko   WA: Life
Agbodike   Ibo: The lineage is a powerful one
Agboji   Ibo: One of strong lineage

Agbomma   Ibo: A beautiful race
Agboola   Yoruba: Circle of honor
Aghadiegwu   Ibo: War is terrible
Aghajiuba   Ibo: War prevents wealth
Agibor   EA: Born in the wet season
Agodichinma   WA: As it pleases God
Agu   WA: Lion
Aguiyi   Ibo: Crocodile
Agunbiade   Yoruba: One who is erect like a crown
Agunna   Ibo: Strong boy
Agunwanyi   Ibo: Strong woman
Aguocha   Ibo: White leopard
Aguwa   Ibo: Terror of the world
Agwamba   Ibo: The custom of a people
Agwubuiro   Ibo: The devil is our enemy
Agwujindu   Ibo: The great power that preserves life
Ahachukwu   Ibo: God's name
Ahaefuefu   Ibo: A name never dies
Ahaiwe   Ibo: A name that inspires anger
Ahamba   Ibo: The name of a people
Ahiaigbo   Ibo: The market of the Igbo people
Ahiazunwa   Ibo: Children are not bought from the market
Ahlam   NA: Dreams
Ahmed   NA: Ahmada more commendable
Ahmed   NA: More commendable
Ahonja   WA: Prosperity
Ahoto   WA: Peace
Ahuekwe   Ibo: Seeing is believing
Ahumma   Ibo: Beautiful body
Ahunna   Ibo: A child that has his father's body
Ahuodo   Ibo: Yellow skinned
Ahuoma   Ibo: Good body
Ahurole   WA: Loving
Ahuzuomoke   WA: May I be perfectly well
Aida   Swahili: Advantage
Aida   Arabic: Reward
Aidoo   WA: Arrived
Aiffat   Swahili: Virtue
Aina   Yoruba: Surrounded by mystery
Aisha   EA: She is life

Aisha   Swahili: Alive
Aishah   Arabic: Prosperous
Aiyetoro   WA: Peace on earth
Ajaegbum   Ibo: No juju will hurt you
Ajagu   Ibo: Sacrifice that demands the use of a Leopard
Ajakaye   Yoruba: Universal struggle
Ajala   WA: Dedicated to the God Ala
Ajamu   Hausa: God of strength
Ajandu   Ibo: Sacrifice that will bring life
Ajani   Yoruba: Someone possessed through struggle
Ajayi   WA: Born face downwards
Ajene   WA: True
Ajibike   Yoruba: One who wakes up to find care
Ajidagba   Yoruba: One who becomes an elder right from youth
Ajike   Ibo: Stength
Ajisafe   Yoruba: Pacesetter (usually of fashion trends)
Ajla   Swahili: Fast
Ajoke   Yoruba: One whom we are all to favor
Ajuluchukwu   WA: Asked of God
Ajunwa   Ibo: The consolation of a child
Ajuonuma   Ibo: Antidote for wrath
Akabbueze   WA: Support is paramount
Akabude   Ibo: One may become famous by one's deeds
Akabueze   Ibo: King by his own making
Akabuogu   Ibo: Fist fights are for strong men
Akabuokwu   Ibo: One's handiwork may bring one trouble
Akachi   Ibo: Hand of God Also Akachuku
Akaegbe   Ibo: The handwork of a gun
Akajiaku   Ibo: A wealthy man
Akajioke   Ibo: An enterprising man
Akajiuka   Ibo: One who disrupts a conversation
Akamafula   WA: May my work be rewarded
Akanbi   Yoruba: A child born with a touch
Akandu   Ibo: Thought of life
Akanika   Yoruba: Born during the festival
Akanni   Yoruba: A child concieved by touch
Akanue   Ibo: It is heard when it is said
Akaola   Ibo: The hand that makes money
Akaoma   Ibo: Good hands
Akarandu   Ibo: The cord of life

Akatwijuka   Uganda: God alone
Akbar   NA: Greater
Akenke   Yoruba: Precious daughter
Akeredolu   Yoruba: One who in spite of being small becomes sucessful
Akerele   Yoruba: One who in spite of being small is strong and touch
Akida   NA: Belief
Akiki   Uganda: Ambassador
Akilah   Arabic: Bright
Akili   NA: Intelligence
Akili   WA: Wisdom
Akili   Ibo: Born strong
Akinbiyi   Yoruba: A bold man gave birth to this
Akinlabi   Yoruba: Product of a brave man
Akinluyi   Yoruba: Valour is dignity
Akinola   Yoruba: Valour of high status
Akintunde   WA: A bravery man has come
Akinwunmi   WA: I like bravery man
Akinyele   Yoruba: A valiant man confers dignity on a house
Akinyemi   Yoruba: Valour befits me
Akna   WA: Born on Thursday
Ako   WA: The first child
Akobundu   Ibo: One survives by prudence
Akomolafe   Yoruba: One who teaches young men gallant ways
Akonye   Ibo: Who is being abused
Akos   Akan: Born on Sunday
Akosua   Ghana: Born on Sunday
Akpagu   Ibo: Bag of leopad skin
Akpamgbo   Ibo: Bag of bullets
Akponye   Ibo: Who is being taken along
Akram   NA: More generous
Akua   WA: Sweet messenger
Akuabia   Ibo: Wealth has arrived
Akuako   WA: Younger of twins
Akubata   Ibo: May wealth increase
Akubuiro   Ibo: Wealth brings enemies
Akubuokwu   Ibo: One's wealth may be a source of trouble
Akuchukwu   Ibo: Wealth from God
Akuegbueze   Ibo: Riches do not kill a king
Akueze   Ibo: Wealth of a King
Akuj   EA: High God

Akumam   Ibo: May health come my way
Akumiwa   WA: Brave
Akunna   Ibo: Father's wealth
Akunne   Ibo: Mother's wealth
Akunwa   Ibo: Child's wealth
Akuoha   Ibo: Public wealth
Akwaeke   Ibo: Eggs of a boa
Akwaoma   Ibo: Good cloth
Akwate   WA: Elder of twins
Akwete   WA: Younger of twins
Al-farid   NA: the unique religious reformer
Al-Tarik   Arabic: Popular name in Kuwait and Saudi Arabia
Alaafin   Yoruba: Lord of the palace
Alaba   WA: Born after Idowu
Alabuike   Ibo: The soil is powerful
Alachem   Ibo: May the soil watch over me
Alade   Yoruba: Crowned one
Aladinma   WA: I am happy with my stay
Aladum   Ibo: The earth goddess leads me
Alaeze   Ibo: The land of the noble
Alaezi   Ibo: Outside land
Alagboogu   Ibo: May the earth goddess bring fighting to a stop
Alaiche   Ibo: Land that is different
Alajindu   Ibo: Ala is the center of life
Alake   Yoruba: Lord of Ake
Alakija   Yoruba: Lord of Ikija
Alakweeme   Ibo: If the earth consents it happens
Alakwemma   Ibo: May the earth goddess permit good things
Alakwenu   Ibo: Let the land permit
Alakwenwa   Ibo: Ala permits population growth
Alakwenze   Ibo: Ala protect the leaders
Alalade   Yoruba: White cloth worn for worship
Alama   Swahili: Sign
Alamenjo   Ibo: Ala knows who does evil
Alamini   NA: Trustworthy
Alaoma   Ibo: Good earth
Alaopa   Yoruba: Plentiful harvest
Alayande   Yoruba: Here comes the master drummer
Alazom   Ibo: May the earth goddess defend me
Albert   English: Noble and brilliant

Alero   Shekiri: The earth is fertile
Alexander   Greek: Defender and helper of humankind
Alhaadi   NA: Guide
Ali   NA: Exalted
Aligwekwe   Ibo: One yields after resistance unprofitable
Alike   Yoruba: She is my favorite
Alile   Yao: She weeps; Alili
Alima   Arabic: Cultured
Alimayu   EA: God is honored
Aliya   Swahili: Exalted
Aliyah   Arabic: Exalted
Alochukwukamma   Ibo: God's plan is the best
Alonnakamma   Ibo: Father's plan is the best
Alonzo   English: Form of Alphonso
Aloysius, Louis   Latin: The very wise
Aluma   WA: Come here
Alvin   English: Noble friend
Alzena   Arabic: Woman
Ama   Ibo: Compound
Ama   WA: Born on Saturday
Ama   Ghana: Born on Saturday
Amaad   NA: Support
Amachukwu   Ibo: God's witness
Amadi   Ibo: Dedicated to the God Amadi
Amadi   Ibo: Giant; one who stands tall
Amadoma   Akan: Born on Saturday
Amaechi   Ibo: Nobody knows tomorrow
Amaechi   WA: Who knows the future?
Amaechiechi   Ibo: The kindred will not discontinue
Amaefuefu   Ibo: The family will not fade away
Amajuoyi   Ibo: The family compound will not become desolate
Amal   NA: Hope
Amali   Swahili: Hope
Amana   Swahili: Trust
Amanambu   WA: You can't tell from the start
Amanchechi   WA: who knows God's will
Amani   NA: Peace
Amani   Arabic: Aspiration
Amanwachi   Ibo: Nobody knows who will be the favorite child of God
Amanze   Ibo: The compoud of a king

Amaogechukwu   Ibo: Who knows God's time?
Amaogechukwu   WA: No one knows God's time
Amar   NA: Long life
Amarachi   Ibo: God's grace
Amatefe   WA: Born after father's death
Amaucheckukwu   Ibo: Who knows God's plan
Amauchenna   Ibo: Who knows father's plan
Amaucheoha   Ibo: Who knows the will of the people
Amaugo   Ibo: Powerful compound
Amauza   WA: Who knows the way
Amauzochukwu   Ibo: Who knows the ways of God
Amazu   WA: Can't know everything
Ambakisye   WA: God is merciful to me
Ambar   NA: Ambergris
Ambe   WA: We begged God for it
Ambrose   Greek: (Αμβροσος) Immortal, divine
Ame   NA: Universal
Amevi   WA: Child of a human being
Amin   NA: Honest
Amina   EA: She is trustworthy
Amina   Swahili: Faithful
Aminah   Arabic: Honest
Aminata   WA: Good character
Amini   NA: Trustworthy
Amira   NA: Queen
Amira   Swahili: Princess
Amiri   NA: Prince
Amma   WA: Famous
Amne   Swahili: Secure
Amonke   WA: To know her is to pet her
Amos   Biblical: Troubled
Ampah   WA: Trust is supreme
Amra   Swahili: Lasting power
Amran   NA: Prosperity
Amunike   Ibo: One who possesses supernatural strength
Anan   WA: Fourth born
Anapa   WA: Morning
Anasa   NA: Entertainment
Anastasia   Greek:: (Αναστασια) Resurrection; Annastasia, Anastashia
Andaiye   EA: A daughter comes home

Anderson   English: Son of Andrew; Andre
Andrew   Greek: (Ανδρεας) Manly; Andy
Aneesa   Swahili: Companion
Anferne   African-American name Originated from Ibo; Anaemefe
Angelo   Greek: (Αγγελος) Messenger, angel
Anifalaje   Yoruba: One who has Ifa and has prosperity
Anika   WA: Goodness
Anisa   Swahili: Friendly; Anisun
Anjorin   Yoruba: We usually move around together
Ankoma   WA: Last born of parents
Ano   WA: The second child
Antar   NA: Hero
Anthony   Latin: Worthy of great praise
Antoine   French; German Anton
Anuabunwa   Ibo: Animal is no substitute for a child
Anuli   WA: Joy
Anuonye   Ibo: Who is glad of whose situation in life
Anwar   NA: Bright
Anwar   NA: more light
Anwar   NA: Shiny
Anwuruoku   Ibo: Nuisance value
Anyachi   Ibo: The watchful eyes of God
Anyadibia   Ibo: The perceptive eye of the diviner
Anyadiegwu   Ibo: The watchful eye shoul be dreaded
Anyadire   Ibo: The watchful eye is effective
Anyaegbuibe   Ibo: No one can destroy others by their look
Anyaegbum   Ibo: I will not be destroyed by the envious eyes
Anyairo   Ibo: Hateful eyes
Anyaleike   Ibo: People should marvel at what power strength can do
Anyalemma   Ibo: May the eye always be directed towards the good
Anyandu   Ibo: Eyes of life
Anyanna   Ibo: Father's eyes
Anyanwu   WA: Dedicated to the God
Anyaogu   Ibo: The undiscriminating eye
Anyaoma   Ibo: Good eyes
Anyarogbum   Ibo: The sneer of an evil will not hurt you
Anyaudo   Ibo: Peaceful eye
Anyaugo   Ibo: The noble eye
Anyauwa   Ibo: Eyes of the world
Araba   Akan: Born on Tuesday

Arafa   Swahili: Knowledgeable
Archibald   Greek: (Αρχιβαλδης) Forrunner; Archie - short form
Aribisala   Yoruba: One who finds a place to run to for safety
Arif   NA: Knowledgeable
Arifa   Swahili: Knowledgeable
Arike   Yoruba: One who only needs to be seen to be petted
Aris   Greek: A prefix for words like Aristocratic, Aristos
Ariyo   Yoruba: One whom men rejoice to see
Armstead   English: A Popular name in the African American community
Arogundale   Yoruba: One who on seeing the battle puts on the crown
Arsenio   Greek: (Αρσενικο) The masculine one
Arthur   English: Noble
Arusi   WA: Born during wedding
Arvarh   Turkish: Unknown
As'ad   NA: happier
Asa   Biblical: Healer
Asa   NA: Life is given
Asa   WA: The third child
Asabi   WA: Of select birth
Asabi   Yoruba: One chosen to be born
Asad   NA: Lion
Asake   Yoruba: One chosen for petting
Asama   Swahili: Exalted
Asani   NA: Rebellious
Asante   NA: Beign good
Asatira   Swahili: Legend
Asesimba   Swahili: Born in nobility
Asesimba   WA: Noble birth
Asghar   NA: Younger
Asha   EA: She is life; Ashia
Asha   Swahili: : Life in wealth
Ashaki   WA: Beautiful
Ashford   English: Dweller at the ash tree
Ashley   English: From the ash tree meadow
Ashraf   NA: Noble
Ashton   English: From the ash tree farm
Ashur   NA Born in the first ten days of Muharram
Ashura   Swahili: companion
Asiegbum   Ibo: People's hatred will not destroy me
Asila   Swahili: noble origin

Asiya   Swahili: Console
Asma   Arabic: Precious
Asmahani   Swahili: Exalted
Asong   WA: Seventh born
Asonye   Ibo: Who is being feared
Assitou   WA: Careful
Asumini   Swahili: Jasmine
Asura   EA: Born during month of Ashur
Asya   EA: Overcomes by grief
Ata   WA: Twin
Atakpa   WA: If you eat me you'll die
Ategar   EA: Tribes man
Athumani   NA The third Khalifa
Atiba   WA: Understanding
Atif   NA: Compassionate
Atiya   Swahili: gift
Ato   EA: This one is brilliant
Atsu   WA: Younger of twins
Atsufi   WA: Born twin
Atta   Akan: Twin
Atu   WA: Born on Saturday
Atuchukwu   Ibo: A sign from God
Atuegbu   WA: Fearless
Atuegbuibe   Ibo: Comparison does no harm to anybody
Atuenyi   Ibo: Comparison cannot be made with an elephant
Atueyichukwu   Ibo: Comparison cannot be made with God
Atuoma   Ibo: A good example
Atuonwu   Ibo: Something with which to compare death
Atwooki   Uganda: She is beautiful
Awali   Ibo: Joyful
Awena   Swahili: Gentle
Awi EA: Home person
Awolalu   Yoruba: Divination saves a city
Awolowo   Yoruba: The cult has respect
Ayah   WA: Bright
Ayan   EA: Bright
Ayanna   EA: Beautiful flower
Ayanna   Swahili: She is a beautiful flower
Ayelagbe   Yoruba: It is the world
Ayele   EA: Powerful

Ayeola WA: Rainbow
Ayinde WA: He came after our praises
Ayo Yoruba: Joy
Ayoade Yoruba: Joy of a crown
Ayobami Yoruba: I am blessed with joy
Ayobunmi WA: Joy is given to me
Ayobunni Yoruba: Joy
Ayodeji Yoruba: Joy becomes two
Ayodele WA: Joy comes home
Ayofemi Yoruba: Joy
Ayoka Yoruba: One surrounded with joy
Ayoluwa WA: Joy of our people
Ayoola Yoruba: Joy of high status
Ayoola Ibo: Celebration
Ayubu NA: Job
Ayzize SA: Let it come
Aza Swahili: powerful
Azaan NA: Strength
Azagba WA: Born out of town
Azikiwe WA: Healthy
Aziz NA: Precious
Aziza EA: The child is gorgeous
Aziza Swahili: Precious
Azubugwu Ibo: People behind one confer respect
Azubuike Ibo: Support is strength
Azubuine Ibo: Support confer pride
Azudimma Ibo: It is good to have followers
Azuka WA: Support is paramount
Azukaego Ibo: Children are more vluable than money
Azunna Ibo: What comes after father
Azunwa Ibo: What comes with a child
Azuogu Ibo: The consequences of a fight
Azuonye Ibo: One's back

B

Baaba   Akan: Born on Thursday
Baakir   NA: Eldest
Baako   WA: First born
Baba   NA: Father
Baba   Fante: Born on Thursday
Bababunmi   Yoruba: Father gave me
Babafemi   WA: Father loves me
Babalola   Yoruba: Honor thy father
Babatola   Yoruba: Fathers are enough to boast about
Babatu   WA: Peace maker
Babatunde   WA: Father reincarnates
Babayeju   Yoruba: Fathers confer dignity on children's outlook
Babechi   NA: Father
Babirye   Uganda: Elder twin sister
Babu   EA: A doctor
Badawi   NA: Nomad
Baderinwa   Yoruba: Worthy of respect
Badilini   NA: Change
Badrak   NA: He has mercy
Badrani   NA: Moon-like
Badriya   Swahili: Moonlike
Badru   WA: Born at full moon
Badu   WA: Tenth born
Baha   NA: Brilliance
Bahari   NA: One who sails
Bahati   EA: My fortune is good
Bahati   Swahili: Luck
Bahati   WA: Luck
Bahiya   Swahili: Beautiful

Baka   NA: Permanence or abbreviation of Bakari
Bakari   NA: First born
Bakhitah   NA: Fortunate
Balagun   WA: Warlord
Banasa   WA: Born on Monday
Bandele   WA: Follow me home
Banga   SA: Sharp as a knife
Bangadabo   WA: Discord in the family
Baraka   NA: blessings
Barghash   NA: Sultan of Zanzibar
Barke   Swahili: Blessings
Basel   NA: Bravery is his prize
Basha   Swahili: Act of God
Bashaam   Swahili: Rich
Bashira   Swahili: Predictor of good news
Bashiri   NA: Predictor
Basil   Greek: (Βασιλης) Of royalty
Basma   Swahili: Smile
Bassey   English: Of royalty; popular with the Calabar tribe of Nigeria
Batholomew   Biblical: Farmer's son; one of the 12 apostles
Batuuli   Swahili: Maiden
Bausi   NA: Sharpener of knives
Bavuai NA: Fisherman
Baya   Swahili: Ugly
Baye   WA: Straightforward
Bayo   WA: There is joy
Bayo   Yoruba: Joy is found
Bayyina   Swahili: Evidence
Bebi   Swahili: Baby
Beduwa   Akan: The tenth child
Bejide   Yoruba: Girl born during a rain storm
Bekitemba   SA: One you can trust
Belewa   WA: Happiness
Beluchi   WA: Provided God approves
Beluonwu   WA: Provided death does not overtake us
Benjamin   Biblical: Fortunate
Bernard   German: Brave as a bear
Bertrand   German: Bright shield
Betserai   SA: Sent to comfort
Beyioku   Yoruba: If this one does die

Bhoke   EA: He wanders the land
Bia   Swahili: Home
Bilal   NA: Trustworthy
Bilali   NA: Stood a test
Bilqisi   Swahili: Queen of Sheba
Bimbaya   Swahili: Ugly lady
Bimkubwa   Sudan: A great lady
Bimkubwa   Swahili: Older lady
Bimnono   Swahili: Fat lady
Bina   NA: My favorite
Bindogo   Swahili: Young lady
Binta   WA: Beautiful daughter
Biobaku   Yoruba: He did not die
Birago   WA: sensible
Birungi   Uganda: Nice
Bisa   WA: Gently loved
Bishara   Swahili: Good news
Bisuga   Yoruba: One born into a palace
Bitisururu   Swahili: Daughter that will bring happiness
Bititi   Swahili: Strong lady
Biubwa   Swahili: Soft and smooth
Bobo   WA: Be humble
Bolade   Yoruba: Honor arrives
Bolanile   WA: The wealth of this house
Bolanile   Yoruba: She is the wealth of her home
Bolodeoku   Yoruba: The the market master does not die
Boma   NA: Fortress
Bomani   EA: A mighty soldier
Bongani   SA: Sing with joy
Boniswa   SA: That which has been unveiled
Boraafya   NA: Better health
Boris   Russian: Warrior Boris Yeltsin, president of Russia
Borishade   WA: She respects the deities
Bosede   WA: Born on Sunday
Bryant   Irish: Strong or virtuous
Bunmi   WA: My gift
Bunmi   Yoruba: My gift
Bunwi   WA: My gift
Bupe   WA: Hospitality
Bupe   Nyakyusa: Hospitality

Burhaan   NA: Proof
Burnell   Irish: Brown skin
Buruku   WA: Named after the deity Buruku
Buseje   Yao: Ask me
Bushira   Swahili: Announcer of good news
Bushiri   NA: Predictor
Butu   WA: Weary
Bwerani   WA: Welcome
Byron   English: A place name meaning barn for cows

C

Cacanja   EA: A medicine priest
Calinikos   Greek: (Καλινικος) Sweet victory
Calvin   Latin: Bald one
Camara   WA: One who teaches from experience
Camara   Cameroon: Teacher
Carlisle   English: One from the fortified city Carlos Spanish form
Carroll   Irish: Champion
Carter   English: A cart driver
Carvel   English: From the estate in the marshes
Carver   English: A wood carver
Cassius   Latin: Vain
Cato   Latin: Knowledgable
Cazembe   CA: He is a wise man
Cecil   Latin: Blind one
Chacha   NA: Strong
Chaga   NA: Holiday
Chandu   NA: Octopus
Changa   CA: Strond as iron
Changamire   CA: He is as the sun
Chaonaine   Ogoni: She has seen me
Charakupa   WA: That which you are given
Charles   German: Strong and manly Charlie A form of Charles
Chatha   WA: An ending
Chatuluka   WA: A departure
Chausiku   EA: Born at night

Chausiku Swahili: Born at night
Chausiku WA: Born at night
Cheche Swahili: Small thing
Chenzira SA: Born to the road
Chenzira WA: Born on the road
Chester Latin: Fortress
Chewa SA: A strong tribe
Chiaku Ibo: God of wealth
Chiamaeze Ibo: God is no respector of persons
Chiamaka WA: Chi is splendid
Chiamaka WA: God is splendid
Chiamaobi Ibo: God is not bound by the individual wishes
Chianakwem Ibo: God will never prevent good things coming my way
Chibale WA: Kingship
Chibueze Ibo: Personal god is the ruler
Chibumma Ibo: Chi/personal god brings well-being
Chibuoke Ibo: Chi/personal God makes one famous
Chicha WA: Beloved
Chidi Ibo: Chi exists
Chidi Ibo: That God exists is proven by the things he does
Chidi WA: God exists
Chidike Ibo: God is strenght
Chidimma Ibo: God is good
Chidubem WA: May God lead me
Chiechefum Ibo: God will never forget me
Chiechefunwa Ibo: May God not forget the child
Chiegenti Ibo: God does not listen to the enemy
Chiehiura Ibo: God does not sleep
Chiemeka WA: God has done much
Chiganu WA: Hound
Chigbogu Ibo: May God provide a solution
Chijibe Ibo: To Gid belongs all gifts
Chijioke Ibo: God bestows blessings
Chika Ibo: Chi is supreme
Chike Ibo: God of strength
Chikezie WA: My God create well
Chikozi WA: The reck
Chiku Swahili: Charterer
Chikwendu WA: Life depends on God
Chimaelu Ibo: God knows everything

Chimaisi   NA: Young and proud
Chimamga   WA: Maize
Chimma   Ibo: Luchy one
Chimodu   Ibo: God the protector
Chimuanya   Ibo: God is awake
Chimuche   Ibo: Human thoughts cannot be hidden from God
Chimwala   Yao: A stone
Chinangwa   WA: Cassava
Chinasaokuru   Ibo: God answers for me
Chineke   Ibo: God the Creator
Chinenye   Ibo: Chi gives
Chinjo   Swahili: Slaughter
Chinoso   Ibo: God is near
Chinouyazura   WA: Will return
Chinua   Ibo: God's own
Chinwe   Ibo: It belongs to God
Chinyelu   WA: Invincible
Chinyere   Ibo: God is the giver
Chioma   Ibo: One with good luck
Chioma   Ibo: The good
Chioneso   SA: Guiding light
Chiosa   Ibo: God of all
Chipe   Swahili: Sprout
Chipo   SA: Great gift
Chipo   WA: Gift
Chipo   Shona: A gift
Chitoom   Ibo: May God praise me
Chiudo   Ibo: The God of peace
Chiugo   Ibo: The noble God
Chizoba   Ibo: May Chi perfect
Chizom   Ibo: May my god protect me
Chotsani   Yao: Take away
Christopher   Greek: (Χριστοφορος) One who carries Christ in his heart
Chuck   NK: for Charles
Chuike   EA: She brings peace in time of trouble
Chuki   Swahili: Resentment
Chukwunyeaka   Ibo: May God help
Chukwubike   Ibo: One with God is strong
Chukwubuanuri   Ibo: God brings happiness
Chukwubueze   Ibo: God is king

Chukwubundu Ibo: One with God has life
Chukwubunna Ibo: God is fatherly
Chukwubunrasiobi Ibo: It is God who alone can console
Chukwubuogwu Ibo: God provides remedy
Chukwubuzo Ibo: God is the way
Chukwuchomma Ibo: Let God make me beautiful
Chukwudiebere Ibo: God the merciful
Chukwudiegwu Ibo: God is to be feared
Chukwudielu Ibo: God is the Highest
Chukwudigboo Ibo: God is omnipotent
Chukwudike Ibo: God is powerful
Chukwudinka Ibo: Skillful
Chukwudiomimi Ibo: God is deep
Chukwudum Ibo: May God guide me
Chukwuekwenjo Ibo: God will not permit evil
Chukwugbamizu Ibo: May God whisper to me
Chukwugbogu Ibo: May God intervene to resolve the issue
Chukwujamma Ibo: May God bless
Chukwujianuli Ibo: To God belong happiness to give out
Chukwujindu Ibo: God depend on all life
Chukwujiofo Ibo: To God belong equitable judgment
Chukwukweanu Ibo: Chukwu if God permits we will know
Chukwukwuougwo Ibo: May God give the reward
Chukwumeuche Ibo: May God's will be done
Chukwundinso Ibo: Chukwunonso God is always near me
Chukwunwekele Ibo: To God be the glory
Chukwunwemma Ibo: Beauty belongs to God
Chukwunwendu Ibo: All life belongs to God
Chukwunwengozi Ibo: All blessings come from God
Chukwunweolu Ibo: Achievement comes as a gift of God
Chukwunweugwo Ibo: Reward comes from God
Chukwunwewa Ibo: Children belong to God
Chukwunweze Ibo: God bestows kingship
Chukwunwike Ibo: Strength comes from God
Chukwunwoha Ibo: All people belong to God
Chukwunwuche Ibo: All wisdom comes from God
Chukwunwude Ibo: Fame comes from God
Chukwunyeaka Ibo: May God send help
Chukwunyeaku Ibo: May God give wealth
Chukwusoom Ibo: May God not expose me

Chukwuzaoku Ibo: May God answer our prayer
Chukwuzeeiwe Ibo: May God soften his anger
Chukwuzua Ibo: May God feed me
Chum NA: Black
Chuma NA: Iron, strong
Chuma WA: God knows
Chuma WA: Wealth
Clarence Latin: Illustrious
Clark English: A clergyman
Claude Latin: Lame
Clay German: To stick together
Clement Latin: Merciful one, gentle
Cleon Latin: Renowned father
Cleopatra Famous Egyptian queen
Colby English: The dark-haired one
Coleman English: Dove
Colin Irish: Young and manly
Congo, Koungo by the wale tribe in Zaire A warrior's name
Conroy Irish: Wise adviser
Cornell, Cornelius: Popular figure in roman mythology
Courtney English: One who dwells in the courts
Craig Scottish: One who dwells at rocky places
Crawford English: Derived from the crow and ford
Cudjoe Ghana: Used to identify freed blacks
Cufee Ghana: (pronounced Kofi) meaning Friday
Cullen Irish: Handsome
Curtis French: Courteous, court bred
Cyril French: Lordly Popular with WA parents
Cyrus Persian: Sun, throne

D

Dada WA: A child with curly hair
Dada Yoruba: She has curly hair
Dagandark NA: sky
Dahoma NA: Long life
Daib EA: She is excellent

Daib   WA: Excellent
Dakar   EA: One community
Dalali   Swahili: Broker
Dalia   WA: Gentle
Dalila   EA: Gentleness is her soul
Dalila   Swahili: Gentle
Dalili   Swahili: Signs
Dalmar   WA: Versale
Dalton   English: A valley town
Damamli   EA: A beautiful vision
Damani   WA: Thoughtful
Damu   NA: blood
Daniel   Biblical: God is my judge. Short form - Danny
Danjuma   WA: Born on Friday
Danladi   WA: Born on Sunday
Daraja   NA: Bridge, stage
Darweshi   NA: Dervish
Darwin   English: A dear friend
Dau   NA: Abbreviation of Daudi
Daud   NA:David
Daudi   NA: David
David   Biblical: Beloved King David was blessed of God
Davin   Scandinavian: Bright, intelligent
Daw   NA: Light
Dawa   Swahili: Medicine
Dawson   English: A surname of earlier centuries
Dayo   Yoruba: Joy has arrived
Dean   English: A valley
Dedan   EA: He loves the city
Deinaba   Calabar: Keep your eye on the ground
Deionogo   Calabar: Always on time. Short form - Deion
Deiriai   EA: Child of the dry season
Deka   WA: She who pleases
Delano   French: Night time
Delbert   English: Noble and brilliant
Delmar   Latin: Belonging to the sea
Delroy   French: The king
Delumo   Yoruba: The crown is knowledge
Delvin (Δελφινι)   Greek: A dolphin
Delwyn   English: Proud friend

Demarre   Of AA creation
Demetrius   Greek: (Δημητριος) Belonging to Demeter, Jimmy short form
Denzel   English: A place in Cornwall
Derby or Darby popular among free black parents
Derek, Derrick   German: The people's ruler
Desmond   English: Gracious protector; Rev. Desmond Tutu of SA
Dhakiya   Swahili: Intelligent
Dhambizao   Swahili: Sinners
Dhoruba   NA: Sterm
Dhuriya   Swahili: Descendant
Dia   WA: Champion
Diallo   WA: Bold
Diarra   WA: Gift
Dibia   WA: Healer
Dibuaku   Ibo: A husband is wealth
Dibugo   Ibo: A woman's glory lies in her husband
Dibuihe   Ibo: Husband is important
Dibumma   Ibo: It is the husband that makes a woman beautiful
Diego A Spanish name for James meaning the supplanted
Digbugwu   Ibo: Husband constitutes a woman's respect
Diji   WA: Farmer
Dike   WA: Warrior, brave
Dikejiaku   Ibo: The courageous are also the wealth
Dikeledi   Tswana: Tears
Dila   NA: Courage
Diliza   SA: Destroyer of evil
Dimgba   Ibo: Skillful wrestler
Dingane   SA: One in time of need
Dinne   Ibo: Husband of her mother
Diochi   Ibo: Skilled wine tapper
Diogu   Ibo: Expert warrior
Dionysus Greek: (Διονισιος) The god of wine and revelry; used as Denis
Diop   CA: Ruler, scholar
Djenaba   WA: Affectionate
Do Ghana: First child following twins
Dodo   Swahili: Lovable
Dodos   Turkana: My friend
Dofi   Ghana: Second child following twins
Dogo   NA: Small
Dolapo   Yoruba: High class

Doli Swahili: Doll
Dominic Latin: Belonging to God; Also Dominick
Dominique The French form of Dominic
Donald Irish: Brown stranger Short form Don, Donnie
Donkor WA: A humble person
Donovan Irish: Dark warrior
Dorian Greek: (Δωρος)Gift Also Dorion, Dorien, Dorean
Doto Swahili: One of the twins
Doto WA: Second of twins
Douglas Scottish: Black water
Douye Yoruba: We got what we sought
Drake Greek: (Δρακος) Dragon
Dridzienyo WA: Birth is good
Ducha Swahili: Little
Dude: Of AA Invention
Duguma WA: Sharp as a spear
Duke French: A leader
Duku Akan: The eleventh born
Dukuzumurenyi WA: Praise to God
Dumisani SA: Forerunner
Dumisani WA: Herald of truth
Dunduza CA: He will venture to see
Duni Swahili: Small
Durah Swahili: Pearl
Durant Latin: The enduring one
Durojaiye WA: Wait and enjoy the word
Durra Swahili: Large pearl
Durueke Ibo: The chief creator
Duruji WA: Farmer
Dwayne Irish: Little dark one
Dyese CA: This is my fortune
Dzidodo WA: Suited for suffering
Dzidzo WA: Happiness
Dzigbodi WA: Patience
Dziko Nguni: The world

E

Earl   English: A chief or nobleman Irish: A solemn pledge
Earvin   Irish: Handsome
Ebenezer   Biblical: Rock of help
Ebere   Ibo: Mercy
Eberechukwu   Ibo: God's mercy
Eberegbum   Ibo: Kind heartedness will never work against me
Eberendu   Ibo: The grace of life
Ebi   Ibo: Good thought
Ebubokansi   Ibo: False accusation is more harmful than poison
Ebun   Calabar: Gift
Ebun   Yoruba: Gift of God
Echeamma   Ibo: One knows when he thinks
Echeanu   Ibo: One remembers by thinking
Echegwuonwu   Ibo: Does one fear death
Echijiole   Ibo: What tomorrow has in store
Ede   WA: Sweetness
Edem   Calabar: Dedicated to the God Ndem
Edo   WA: Love
Edwin   English: Rich in friendship, prosperous friend
Eebudola   Yoruba: Our ridicule has become a thing of honor
Efia   Fante: Born on Friday
Efie   Akan: Born on Friday
Efioanwan   Calabar: Born on the market day Ofiong
Efua   Akan: Born on Friday
Efua   Benin: Born on Friday
Efuru   WA: Daughter of heaven
Egbebunwa   Ibo: Hawk does not pray on a child
Egoaghonwa   Ibo: Money does not become a child
Egobuaku   Ibo: Money is power
Egobuiwe   Ibo: Wealth incurs hatred for one
Egodi   Ibo: There is money
Egoejuafo   Ibo: No one is satisifed with any amount of money
Egoenyinwa   Ibo: Money is not a substitute for a child
Egondu   Ibo: Money that brings life
Egypt An unusual name for boys Egypt is the cradle of civilization
Ehioze   WA: Above people's jealously
Eintou   WA: Pearl
Ejiikeme   WA: Do not use force

Ejike   Ibo: Is one strong/healthy
Eka   WA: Mother of the earth
Ekador   EA: Enter my heart
Ekanem   WA: Mother of All
Ekeama   WA: Nature is splendid
Ekebihe   Ibo: Creator is great
Ekebunwa   Ibo: It is the creator who brings a child
Ekechi   Ibo: God's creation
Ekechukwu   Ibo: God's creation
Ekedi   Ibo: The existence of the creator is shown by what he does
Ekedimma   Ibo: The creator is gracious
Ekedinna   Ibo: Eke is good
Ekejihe   Ibo: All things belong to the creator
Ekejike   Ibo: Power belongs to the creator
Ekejindu   Ibo: Life belongs to the creator
Ekejinma   Ibo: The creator is responsible for all goodness
Ekejiuba   Ibo: The creator is responsible prosperity
Ekejiuba   WA: God's own wealth
Ekekamadu   Ibo: Eke is superior to man
Ekemma   Ibo: A lucky one
Ekenna   Ibo: The crative work of the father
Ekenwendu   Ibo: Life belongs to the creator
Ekenwoha   Ibo: People belong to the creator
Ekenwuwa   Ibo: The world belongs to the creator
Ekenyeanu   Ibo: If the creator gives it will become known
Eko   Yoruba: Lagos, former capital city of Nigeria
Ekperebundu   Ibo: Prayer sustains life
Ekperechi   Ibo: Praying to God
Ekundayo   WA: Sorrow has turned to happiness
Ekundayo   Yoruba: Weeping becomes joy
Ekuwa   Akan: Born on Wednesday
Ekwuanu   Ibo: It is heard when it is said
Ekwueme   Ibo: Person of integrity
Ekwutosi   WA: Do not speak evil against others
El-Fatih   NA: The conqueror
El-Jamah   NA: Paradise
Elebute   Yoruba: Harbour Master
Eleko   Yoruba: Lord of Eko
Eli   Biblical: The highest Also Ely, Elie
Elijah   Biblical: The Lord is my God

Elisha   Biblical: The Lord is my salvation
Elochukwu   Ibo: God's plan
Elon   WA: God loves me
Elroy   Latin: The king
Elton   English: From the old estate
Elumanjo   Ibo: Heaven knows the evil-doers
Elzey   Slang name of the 19th century
Emeanu   Ibo: It is heard when it is done
Emeche   Ibo: One who acts wisely
Emenike   WA: Do not use force
Emeoba   Ibo: One who becomes rich from hard work
Emile   French: To emulate, to be industrious
Emiloa   Yoruba: Spirit of honor
Emmanuel   Biblical: God is with us Also Immanuel
Emory   French: A variation of Emery
Enam   WA: God gave it to me
Enemwoyi   WA: One who has grace
Eniitan   Yoruba: Story behind a lifetime
Ennis, Innis   Irish: Only choice
Enobakhare   WA: What the chief says
Enoch   Biblical: Dedicated
Enomwoyi   WA: One who has grace, charm
Enwemadu   Ibo: Nobody owns anybody
Enyiamairo   Ibo: Friendship knows no hatred
Enyiazu   Ibo: The unknown friend
Enyinwa   Ibo: Child's friend
Enyo   WA: It is enough for me
Enyonyam   Ghana: It is good for me
Enyonyam   WA: It is good for me
Ephraim   Biblical: Fruitful; one of the two sons of Joseph
Erasmus   Greek: (Ερασμος)Love Popular with the Greeks of Mikonos
Erastos   EA: Loverman
Eriaba   Ibo: One who enjoys his wealth
Eric   Scandinavian: Honorable ruler Also Erich, Erik Enrique Spanish
Eririmma   Ibo: Beautiful thread line
Ernest English: Earnest one Also Earnest Ernie short form
Erondu   Ibo: Plan for life
Erwin   Scottish: Beautiful Also Ervin, Irvin
Eshe   Swahili: Life
Eshe   WA: Life

Eshe   Swahili: Life
Esi   Fante: Born on Sunday
Esinam   WA: God has heard me
Etan   Shekiri: God's love never ceases
Ethan   English: Firm, strong
Etiem   EA: Warm place in my heart
Eugene   Greek: (Ευγενια) Wellborn, polite Eugenio is a Spanish variation
Eura   Greek: Of the universe
Evan   Welsh: Jehovah has shown favor
Evers   English: Derived from Everest
Ewansika   WA: Secrets are not for sale
Ewunike   EA: Like a fragrance
Eyidiya   Ibo: Friend of a husband
Eze   Ibo: King
Ezeama   Ibo: The king that is not of the home people
Ezeamaka   Ibo: King is splendid
Ezeanuokwu   Ibo: The king has listened/agreed
Ezebuchi   Ibo: The kings has as much influence on one as one's chi
Ezebugwu   Ibo: Kingship confers prestige/respect
Ezebuike   Ibo: The king is source of strength
Ezebuiro   Ibo: To be king is to breed enemies/hatred
Ezechukwu   Ibo: King ordained by God
Ezedimma   Ibo: The king is good
Ezedinbu   Ibo: A king has always existed
Ezeigwe   Ibo: King of the heavens
Ezejiaku   Ibo: A wealthy king
Ezejiegwu   Ibo: The king is to be feared
Ezejindu   Ibo: The king protects life
Ezejiofo   Ibo: The king exercises justice
Ezekial   Biblical: God will strengthen Also Ezekiel
Ezenachi   WA: The king rules
Ezendu   Ibo: King of life
Ezenna   Ibo: His father's king
Ezenwanyi   Ibo: Lady queen
Ezenwata   Ibo: king with a heart
Ezenwudo   Ibo: The king guarratees peace
Ezenyem   Ibo: May the king bless me
Ezeocha   Ibo: Light skinned king
Ezeoha   Ibo: King of all
Ezeoha   WA: The people's king

Ezeonu   Ibo: King by mouth
Ezewuogo   Ibo: Honor belongs to the king
Eziaku   Ibo: Good wealth
Ezichem   Ibo: May the earth guide us
Ezigbo   Ibo: Beloved
Ezigbo   Ibo: Good people
Eziokwu   Ibo: The Truth
Ezueodi   Ibo: It is good when we are complete

F

Fabayo   WA: A lucky child
Fabayo   Yoruba: A lucky birth is joy
Fabio   Latin: One who works looks fabulous
Fabuluje   Yoruba: Ifa does not ruin a city
Fabunmi   Yoruba: Ifa gave me
Fadairo   Yoruba: Ifa keeps this one waiting
Fadhiila   Swahili: Abundance
Fadhili   NA: Virtuous
Fadilah   Arabic: Virtue
Fadiya   Swahili: Redeemer
Fadwa   Arabic: Sacrifice
Fagbemi   Yoruba: Ifa supported me
Fagbulu   Yoruba: Ifa takes the city
Fagunwa   Yoruba: Ifa straightens character
Fahani   NA: Happy
Fahim   NA: Learned
Fahima   Swahili: Understands
Faida   Swahili: Benefit
Faika   Swahili: Superior
Faiza   Swahili: Victorious
Faizah   Arabic: Victorious
Fakhri   NA: Glory, honor
Fakhta   Swahili: Pierce
Faki   NA: Simple hollow
Fakihi   NA: Wise
Falana   Yoruba: Ifa Cuts a path
Faleti   Yoruba: Ifa adheres to our prayers
Falola   Yoruba: Prestige
Falope   Yoruba: Thanksgiving

Faluyi   Yoruba: Ifa is diginity
Famu   NA: Majesty
Fanta   WA: Beautiful day
Fapohunda   Yoruba: Ifa altered its voice
Faqihi   NA: Wise
Faraji   NA: Consolation
Faraji   WA: Consolation
Farashuu   Swahili: Butterfly
Fari   Wolof: The queen
Farid   NA: Unique
Farida   Swahili: Unique
Faridah   Arabic: Unique
Farihah   Arabic: Joyful
Farjalla   NA: God's consolation
Farlid   NA: Unique
Farrell   Irish: Champion
Farri   NA: A religious man
Faruki   NA: Judicious
Fasaha   Swahili: Eloquence
Fasesin   Yoruba: Ifa is possible to worship
Fashola   Yoruba: God's blessing
Fasuyi   Yoruba: Ifa did us an honor
Fasuyi   Yoruba: Ifa profess diginity
Fathi   NA: Victorious
Fathiya   Swahili: Triumph
Fati   WA: Robust
Fatia   NA: Daughter of the prophet
Fatima   Arabic: Daughter of the prophet
Fatimah   NA: Daughter of the prophet
Fatinah   Arabic: Captivating
Fatoki   Yoruba: Ifa is enough to salute
Fatou   WA: Mata Beloved by all
Fatuma   Swahili: Daughter of the prophet
Fatuma   Swahili: Prophet Muhammad's daughter
Fauzi   NA: Successful
Fauziya   Swahili: Successful
Fayemi   Yoruba: Divination befits me
Fayola   Yoruba: Good fortune
Fayola   Yoruba: Good fortune walks with honor
Febechi   WA: Worship God

Feechi   Ibo: Worship God
Fehed   NA: Panther
Feisal   NA: Arbitrator
Felix   Latin: Happy
Femi   Yoruba: Love me
Fenuku   WA: Born after twins
Ferdinand   German: Bold voyager
Fernando   Spanish: The spanish form of Ferdinand
Feruzi   Swahili: Turquoise
Fidel   NA: Reflect
Fidela   Swahili: Faithful
Fijabi   Yoruba: Born with strife
Fikirini   NA: Reflect
Fila   Swahili: Baldness
Filmore   English: Very famous
Finley   Irish: Brave soldier Also Findley
Firdawsi   Swahili: Beautiful garden
Firyali   Swahili: Extraordinary
Fleming   English: Man from the lowlands
Flint   English: A brook
Floyd   Welsh: Gray-haired
Fogo   NA: High
Fola   Yoruba: Honor
Folade   Yoruba: Honor arrives
Folagbade   Yoruba: Receive a crown with glory
Folami   Yoruba: Respect and honor me
Folashade   Yoruba: Honor gets a crown
Folayan   Yoruba: Walk in dignity
Foluke   Yoruba: Placed in God's care
Foluso   Yoruba: Watch over the child with the help of God
Fontaine   French: A source of water
Ford   English: A road
Foreman   Name given to representatives of the throne
Forrest   Latin: Outdoors
Fortune   Latin: Strong, fortunate
Fouad   NA: Heart
Francesco   Spanish: Frances; Francis
Francis   Latin: Freeman Frank Frank, a pet form of Francis Frantz
Franklin   English: Freeholder
Freddie   AA: Pet name for Frederick

Frederick   German: Peaceful ruler
Freeman   English: One born free
Freya   Swahili: Goddess of love
Fritz   German: A form of Frederick
Fuad   NA: Heart
Fujo   EA: She brings wholeness
Fujo   Yoruba: Born after parent's departure
Fuju   Swahili: Born after parents' separation
Fukayna   Arabic: Studious
Fumiya   Yoruba: Suffering
Fundikira   NA: Learned
Funga   NA: Tie, bind
Furaha   Swahili: Happiness
Fursiya   Swahili: Heroism
Fuvi   WA: A child born into suffering

G

Gabriel   Biblical: God is my strength Gabe A diminutive for Gabriel
Gaika   SA: Gifted in sculpting
Gail   A diminutive for Gaylord
Gamba   SA: He is a warrior
Gamer   NA: Moon
Garfield   English: A surname meaning field of spears
Garnet   Keeper of the grains
Garrett   English: A good spear thrower
Garrick   English: An oak spear
Garth   German: Garden
Gary   German: A spear
Gavin   Welsh: White hawk
Gavivi   WA: Money is good
Gaylor   A jolly fellow
Gbadebo   Yoruba: Bring back the crown
Gbolade   Yoruba: Brought honor It shows, it is visible
Gbolahan   Yoruba: Exibit Honor to return
Gene   A short form of Eugene
Geoffrey   English: The peaceful one
George   Greek: A farmer, one who tills the soil
Gerald   German: Rules by the spear Heraldo in Spanish
Gerard   German: Brave spearman Also Gerrard

Gerisa   EA: Strong as a leopard
Geronimo   Native American: Sacred
Ghadah   Arabic: Beautiful
Ghalib   NA: Winner
Ghalye   Swahili: Swahili: Expensive
Ghaniy   NA: Rich
Ghaniya   Swahili: Rich
Gharib   NA: Stranger, visitor
Gharibuu   Swahili: Stranger
Ghayda   Arabic: Young and delicate
Gheilani   NA: Type of tree
Ghika   Ibo: God is the greatest
Gibson   German: Derived from from Gilbert
Gideon   Biblical: One who cuts down
Gilbert   German: Bright lad
Giles   Greek: (Γιλες) A shield that protects
Gillian   This African-American variation
Gilmore   Scottish: Servant of the Virgin Mary
Ginikanwa   Ibo: What is more precious than a child?
Ginikanwanta   WA: What is more valuable than a child?
Gino   Italian: Gino is a short form of names such as Giovanni
Gladstone   Scottish: From the town near the clearing in the woods
Glendon   Scottish: From the shady valley
Glenn   Irish: From the secluded wooded valley Also Glen, Glyn, Glynn
Glover   English: Glove or paw
Godfrey   English: Of God's peace
Gogo   WA: Like grandfather
Golden   English: pure as gold
Goodman   English: The good man
Goodwin   English: Good, faithful friend
Gordon   English: From the marshes
Goumba   Wolof: Blind
Gowan   Scottish: Wellborn; a variation of Owen
Gowon   WA: Rainmaker
Grady   Irish: A man of rank
Graham   English: One from a farm home
Granger   French: Farmer
Grant   French: Great, tall
Granville   French: The big town
Gray   English: To shine

Grayson   English: The son of an earl
Greg   This short form of Gregory
Gregory   Greek: (Γρηγορος) Vigilant
Griffin   English: Strong and powerful Also Griffith
Guedado   Yoruba: Wanted by no one
Gulai   EA: Born between the rainy seasons
Gunter   German: War Also Gunther
Gus   A short form of Ngozi Used mainly by the Ibos of Nigeria
Guy   Latin: Lively

H

Haamid   NA: Grateful
Habeebah   Swahili: Dear one
Habib   NA: Beloved
Habiba   Swahili: Beloved
Habibka   WA: Sweetheart
Habimama   WA: God exists
Hadiah   NA: Quiet and calm
Hadiya   Swahili: A gift from God
Hadiyah   Arabic: Guide to righteousness
Hadiyyah   Arabic: Gift
Hadley   English: Child from the heather meadow
Hafidh   NA: Preserver
Hafidha   Swahili: Mindful
Hafiz   NA: guardian
Hafsa   Swahili: Sound judgement
Haidar   NA: Strong, stout
Haifa   Swahili: Slim
Haji   NA: Pilgrim
Haki   NA: Right, truth
Hakim   NA: Judge, wise Also Akeem
Hakima   Swahili: Sensible
Hakizimana   WA: Born on Thursday
Hala   Swahili: Glourious
Halali   NA: Cresent
Hale   English: Hero in good health
Haleem   NA: He does not anger
Hali   NA: Condition
Halima   Swahili: Gentle

Halina   WA: Gentle

Hall   English: Dweller at the hall or manor house

Hallam   Arabic: Dweller at the slope

Hamadi   NA: Gracious

Hamdaan   NA: Praise

Hami   NA: Defend

Hamid   NA: Thanking God

Hamida   Swahili: Gracious

Hamilton   English: Beautiful mountain

Hamisi   NA: Born on Thursday

Hamlet   German: Little home

Hammond   English: A home; a form of Hamlet

Hampton   English: Town or village

Hamza   NA: Prophet Muhammad's uncle

Hana   Arabic: Happiness

Hanaa   Swahili: Happiness

Hanif   NA: Resoulte in belief

Hanifa   Swahili: Pure

Hanifah   Arabic: True believer

Haniyyah   Arabic: Happy

Hank   This nickname for Henry

Hanley   English: Meadow

Hannibal   English: A steep hill

Haomyaro   WA: Born during conflicts

Haoniyao   Swahili: Self centered

Haqikah   Arabic: Truthful

Harambe   NA: Let's pull together

Harbuu   Swahili: Warrior

Harcourt   French: A fortified dwelling Nickname Harry

Hardy   German: Strong

Harford   English: From the hare ford

Hark   An unusual name of obscure origins

Harley   English: The meadow of the hares

Harold   English; Army commander

Harper   English: One who plays the harp

Harrell   A Scandinavian form of Harold

Harris   English: Son of Harry Also Harrison

Harry   This nickname for Henry

Hartha   Swahili: Fertile

Harub   NA: Warrior

Haruun   NA: Messenger Also Aharon, Aaron
Harvey   French: Strong and ardent
Hasan   NA: Good
Hasanati   Swahili: Good
Hasanati   Swahili: Merits
Hasani   NA: Good
Hashil   NA: Emigrant
Hashim   NA: Honor
Hasiina   Swahili: Attractive
Hasina   Swahili: Lady
Hasna   Arabic: Beautiful
Hasnaa   Swahili: Beauty
Hasnuu   NA: Handsome
Hassiem   NA: Strong
Hatari   NA: danger
Hauli   NA: Power
Hawa   Swahili: Longing
Hawa   Swahili: Mother of mankind
Hawanya   WA: A tear
Hawthorne   English: One from the field of hawthorns
Hayati, Hayaat   Swahili: Life
Hayes   English: From the hedged place
Hayfa Arabic: Slender, beautiful body
Helal   NA: Like the cresent
Hembadon   WA: The winner
Henry   German: Ruler of the home
Herbert   English: Bright, excellent ruler
Hercules   Greek: (Ηρακλης) Glorious Hercules, the son of Zeus
Herman   German: Soldier
Hezekiah   Biblical: God is my strength
Hiba   Swahili: Gift
Hilliard   Greek: Cheerful Also Hillard Hilly A nickname for Hilliard
Himidi   NA: Grateful
Hindi   NA: Indian, sharp armor
Hiram   Biblical: Of noble birth
Hishaam   NA: Generosity
Hisham   NA: Generous
Hobo   Swahili: Gift
Hobson   English: Son of Robert
Hodari   NA: Expert

Homaleni   SA: Be prepared to defend yourself
Hondo   SA: Warrior
Hondo   WA: War
Horera   Swahili: Kitten
Hosea   Biblical: Salvation
Houston   Scottish: A surname meaning from Hugh's town
Howard   English: Noble watchman Howie A nickname for Howard
Howell   Welsh: Eminent, remarkable
Hubert   German: Bright, shining mind
Huda   Swahili: Guidence
Huddie   African-American invented. Hudd; a pet form of Richard
Hudham   Swahili: Astute
Hugh   English: Intelligent Hughlyn A variation of Hugh
Hujayja   Swahili: Evidence
Humphrey   German: Strength English: Peace
Humud   NA: Gracious
Hunter   English: One who hunts
Huntley   English: From the hunter's meadow
Hununi   Swahili: Cheerful
Hurani   NA: Restive
Huseni   NA: Good A diminutive of Hasan
Huseni   NA: Trustworthy
Husna   Swahili: Beautiful
Husni   NA: Goodness
Huxley   English: A field of ash trees
Hyde   English: A measure of land
Hyder   English: One who prepares hides for tanning
Hyland   English: One who lives in the high lands; Hylan
Hyman: Life

I

Ian   Scottish: God is gracious
Ibahim   WA: Father is exalted
Ibeabuchi   Ibo: People are not God to their neighbors
Ibeamaka   WA: The agnates are splendid
Ibeawuchi   WA: The agnates are not good
Ibebuike   Ibo: One's strength lies in the support of one's kindred

Ibebunjo   Ibo: One's fellows constitute one's danger
Ibeguenyi   Ibo: Neighbors don't hurt each other
Ibekweanu   Ibo: When people agree, there is harmony
Ibekwunma   Ibo: Colleagues never speak well of others
Ibidum   Yoruba: It is sweet
Ibrahim   NA: Ebrahim
Ibrahim   NA: Father
Ibtisam   Swahili: Smile
Ibuchi   Ibo: Are you God?
Ibukunola   Yoruba: Constant acknowledgment
Ichabod   Biblical: The glory is gone
Idi   EA: Born during the Idi festival
Idi   NA: Festivity
Idomenyin   Yoruba: Hope
Idowu   WA: Born after twins
Idriis   NA: Prophet
Idrissa   WA: Immortal
Ife   Yoruba: Love
Ifeakandu   Ibo: There is nothing more valuable than life
Ifeakanwa   Ibo: A child iss the best
Ifeanacho   WA: The desired child
Ifeanyichukwu   Ibo: Nothing impossible for God
Ifeolu   Yoruba: God's love
Ifetayo   Yoruba: Love brings happiness
Ifeyinwa   Ibo: There is nothing similar to a child
Ifoma   Ibo: Goodluck; Also Ifeoma
Igbeaku   Ibo: Box of wealth
Igbekoyi   Yoruba: Bush refused this one
Igboerinwa   Ibo: Everybody does not benefit from a child
Igbojiaku   Ibo: Our people are wealthy
Igboonu   Ibo: Our people are boastul
Ige   Yoruba: Delivered feetfirst
Ignatius   Latin: Fiery one
Igwebuike   Ibo: Heaven is great
Igwedimma   Ibo: Heaven is beautiful
Igwedire   Ibo: There is heaven
Igwedum   Ibo: Heaven lead me
Iheakachi   Ibo: Nothing is greater than God
Iheakanwa   Ibo: Nothing is more important than a child
Ihebuaku   Ibo: Things are valuable

Ihebuzo   Ibo: Forerunner
Ihechi   Ibo: Light of God
Ihechukwu   WA: Light of God
Ihedike   Ibo: Life is hard
Ihedimma   Ibo: Life are good
Ihedinanwa   Ibo: A child is not cheap
Ihegbulam   Ibo: Nothing will kill me
Ihekandu   Ibo: Larger than life
Iheke   Ibo: destiny
Ihekweahu   Ibo: Light of the people
Ihemechi   Ibo: Nothing can effect one's destiny
Ihenendu   Ibo: Life will not be harmed
Iheoma   Ibo: Good natured
Iheuwa   Ibo: Wordly belonging
Iheyinwa   Ibo: All comes through Divine Providence
Ihudi   Ibo: Husband's face
Ihueze   Ibo: The face of the king
Ihuku   Ibo: A face that brings good luck
Ihunna   Ibo: Father's face
Ihuoma   Ibo: Good luck; lucky child
Ijebunka   Ibo: Excercise caution in life's journey
Ijebuonwu   Ibo: Journey can be death
Ijedi   Ibo: Travelling to get married
Ijedimma   Ibo: Ijeoma A sucessful journey
Ijego   Ibo: Journey for money
Ijekweanu   Ibo: We will know if the journey is smooth
Ijeoma   Ibo: A good journey
Ijoma   Ibo: Travel Safely
Ijuedo   Ibo: Journey in search of peace
Ike   This diminutive for Isaac
Ikeagwumba   Ibo: A never weary people
Ikeazomba   Ibo: Might does not save a nation
Ikebude   Ibo: Hard work makes one famous
Ikebugo   Ibo: Hard work brings glory
Ikebugwo   Ibo: There is reward for hard work
Ikechukwu   Ibo: Handwork of God
Ikechukwu   WA: The power of God
Ikedichi   Ibo: God is powerful
Ikedieze   Ibo: Powerful king
Ikedioha   Ibo: People are might

Ikediuwa   Ibo: The power of the world
Ikefuefu   Ibo: Labor will not fail to yield fruits
Ikegwualo   Ibo: One returns when tired
Ikegwuonu   Ibo: May mouth be tired of talking
Ikekachi   Ibo: God is above all power/strength
Ikekpere   Ibo: The Power of prayer
Ikemba   Ibo: The strength of a people
Ikenga   Ibo: Warrior
Ikengachem   Ibo: May Ikenga protect me
Ikenna   Ibo: The power of a father
Ikenna   WA: Father's power
Ikenwoke   Ibo: The power of a man
Ikeogu   Ibo: The effect for fighting
Ikeokwu   Ibo: Ikeoku The Power of word
Ikeolu   Yoruba: God's care
Ikeotunoye   Ibo: The strength of one person
Ikerionwu   Ibo: Death superceded power
Ikeuko   Ibo: Something scarce
Ikodi   Ibo: A friend of the husband
Ikonna   Ibo: Father's friend
Ikonne   Ibo: Mother's friend
Ikpeamaonwu   Ibo: Death is never at fault
Ikpedinso   Ibo: The divine judgment is near
Ikpendu   Ibo: Judgement of life
Ikusegham   Ibo: Peace is better than war
Ikwuakoako   Ibo: One does not lack kindred
Ikwuaku   Ibo: Wealth family
Ikwuazom   Ibo: Neighbors cannot help me
Ikwuechindu   Ibo: Neighbors do not safeguard the life of others
Ikwumma   Ibo: Good relations
Ikwunna   Ibo: Father's relatives
Ikwunne   Ibo: Mother's relatives
Ikwuoma   Ibo: Good relations
Ikwuonwu   Ibo: Lethal abuse
Ilechukwu   Ibo: Reliable God
Ilesanmi   Yoruba: Home benfits me
Ilham   Swahili: Inspiration
Ilumooka   Yoruba: The whole city knows him
Ilyaas   NA: Prophet Elijah, the lord is my God
Imaad   NA: Pillar

Imaan   NA: Faith
Iman   Arabic: Preacher
Imani   Swahili: Faith
Imani   NA: Faithful
Imane   Calabar: Faith will prevail
Imara   Swahili: Firm
Imarogbe   WA: Born into a good family
Imediegwu   Ibo: Pregnancy is wonderful
Immanuel   A form of Emmanuel
Inaani   SA: Who is left at home?
Inambura   SA: Rain mother
Inaya   Swahili: Providence
Inge   Scandinavian: Protection
Ingram   Scandinavian: Raven of peace
Inman   Arabic: Form of Iman
Innis   Scottish: Swahili: Irish: From the island Also Ennis
Instisar   Swahili: Victory
Ira   English: Watchful one
Iredike   Ibo: The tongue is powerful
Ireogbunne   Ibo: Hatred does not kill a mother
Ireoma   Ibo: Sweet Tongue
Ireuwa   Ibo: The tongue of the world
Iroabuchi   Ibo: One's enemy is not his God
Iroagwuike   Ibo: Hatred is never tired
Iroanuka   Ibo: Enemy does not listen to logic
Iroawuchi   WA: Enmity does not come from Chi
Irobuariri   Ibo: Enmity is a source of disgrace
Irodinso   Ibo: Enemies are around
Iroechenma   Ibo: An enemy wishes ill
Iroegbum   Ibo: People's hatred will not kill me
Iroegbunwa   Ibo: Hatred does not kill a child
Iroejindu   Ibo: One's life is not at the mercy of the enemy
Iroezindu   Ibo: Enemy does not show good example
Irokansi   Ibo: Enmity is worse than poison
Irokanulo   Ibo: Enemies are more at home
Irokweabia   Ibo: We will come if the enemy permits
Irommuo   Ibo: The enmity of the spirits
Iromuanya   Ibo: Enemies are watchful
Irononso   Ibo: Enemy are around
Iroulo   Ibo: Enemy at home

Irvin   Irish: Handsome
Irwah   NA: Resolution
Irwin   English: Boar friend
Isa   NA: Jesus
Isaac   Biblical: Laughter; the beloved son born to Abraham
Isaam   NA: Guard
Isadore   Greek: (Ισιδωρος)Gift of Isis, the Egyptian goddess of the moon
Isaiah   Biblical: Salvation of God; an Old Testament prophet
Isama'iil   NA: Prophet, he hears
Ishaaq   NA: Prophet, laughter
Isham   English: From the iron one's estate
Ishmael   Biblical: The Lord will hear
Ishtar   Egyptian:: Rod with fire
Isioma   Ibo: Lucky first
Isiuwa   Ibo: The significance of the world
Islam   NA: Safe, submission to God
Isma'iil   NA: He hears Also Ismail
Isoke   Ibo: A satisfying gift from God
Isoke   Benin: A good gift from God
Israel   Biblical: The name given Jacob by the Lord
Italo   WA: Full of valor
Itidal   Swahili: Symmetry
Ivan   Russian: God is gracious, a form of John
Iverem   Tiv: Blessing
Ives   English: Little archer
Ivory   English: Precious metal
Iwebuka   Ibo: Hatred leads to trouble
Iwegbolu   WA: May anger cease
Iwejianuri   Ibo: Anger is the source of unhappiness
Iwuagwu   Ibo: The law of Agwu
Iwuala   Ibo: The taboos of the land
Iwuanyanwu   Ibo: The taboos of the sun
Iwuchukwu   Ibo: The taboos of God
Iwuchukwu   WA: God's commandment
Iwuji   Ibo: The yam taboos
Iwuoha   Ibo: A law of the people
Iyabo   Yoruba: Mother has come back
Iyiola   Yoruba: Prestige
Izebe   Calabar: Long expected child
Izegbe   Benin: Blessed child

Izera   Turkish: Mountainous
Izuchukwu   Ibo: God's plan
Izuegbum   Ibo: The people's scheming will not hurt me
Izuka   Ibo: The slail of talk
Izundu   Ibo: The plan for life
Izuoha   Ibo: The plans of the people
Izuoma   Ibo: Good advice

J

Jaafar   NA: Small river
Jabali   NA: Strong as a rock
Jabari   WA: Brave
Jabez   Egyptian: Born in pain
Jabir   NA: Restorer
Jabiri   NA: Comforter
Jabulani   WA: Be happy
Jack   Pet name for John Jackie - nickname
Jackson   This surname means son of Jack
Jacob   Biblical: One who holds back Jake A diminutive for Jacob
Jacques   French: A form of Jacob
Jade   German: Precious stone
Jaha   EA: This is dignity
Jaha   NA: Dignified
Jaha   Swahili: Prominence
Jahi   Swahili: Prominence; Jahia
Jamila   Swahili: Beautiful
Jaime   Pet name for James
Jala   Arabic: Lucid
Jalali   NA: High, majesty
Jalil   Arabic: Majesty
Jalili   NA: Exalted, dignified
Jamaadar   NA: Army general
Jamal   NA: Beauty
Jamali   NA: Beauty
James   English: The English form of Jacob
Jamieson   English: Son of James
Jamil   NA: Handsome
Jamila   Swahili: Beautiful

Jamilah   Arabic: Beautiful
Jamili   NA: Handsome
Jamshid   Iran: Persian king, Solomon, Jonas
Jan   Dutch: A form of John
Janna   Swahili: Haven
Japera   Shona: It is done
Jaramogi   EA: He travels often
Jarek   Slavic: January
Jaribu   Swahili: One who tries
Jarmon   German: German Also Jerman
Jaron : To sing, to cry out
Jarrell : This variation of Gerald
Jarrett   English: Brave with a spear
Jarrod   Arabic: To descend Also Jared
Jarvis   English: A conqueror
Jasira   Swahili: Bold
Jason : The Lord is my salvation
Jasper   Persian: A semiprecious gemstone
Jassiem   NA: Strong
Jauhar   Swahili: Sweet
Javan   Biblical: A son of Japeth, Noah's son
Jawaad   NA: Generous
Jawahir   WA: The golden woman
Jawanza   CA: This one is dependable
Jay   Latin: Jay bird
Jean : The French form of John
Jecha : Sunrise
Jedidiah   Biblical: Beloved of the Lord Also Jedediah
Jefar   NA: Recovery
Jeff : A short form of Jeffrey
Jeffrey   English: God's peace. Famous City College professor
Jela   WA: Father in pain at birth
Jelani   NA: Great
Jemila   EA: Beautiful
Jemine   Shekiri: God's wish Also Jemi, as a pet forrm
Jendayi   Shona: Give thanks
Jenebi   NA: Affectionate
Jengo   NA: Building, strength
Jenkin   Flemish: Little John
Jenner   Flemish: A Flemmish variation of John

Jennings   English: A descendant of John

Jerald : A modern spelling of Gerald

Jeremiah   Biblical: God will uplift; a major prophet of the Old Testament

Jeremy : A pet form

Jerome   Greek: A sacred or holy name

Jerrold : A spelling variation for Gerald

Jerry : A diminutive for Jerome or Jeremiah

Jesse   Biblical: The Lord exists; the father of King David

Jethro   Biblical: Preeminence

Jiaku   Ibo: Yam that brings wealth

Jibaru   NA: Unknown

Jibowu   Yoruba: One who wakes up to find an ant

Jibuamare   Ibo: One is a wealthy yam farmer by grace

Jibuego   Ibo: Yam is valuable

Jibueze   Ibo: Possession of yam lifts the status of the owner

Jibuike   Ibo: Power comes from the acquisition of yams

Jibuisi   Ibo: Nothing is more important than yam

Jibunka   Ibo: Yam is acquired by skill

Jibunma   Ibo: Possession of yam brings good things

Jibuugwu   Ibo: The possession of yam acords respect

Jibuulo   Ibo: Yam is the only real possession

Jie   Turkana: Beloved

Jim : Pet name for James; Jimmie

Jina   Swahili: Identity

Jinna   Ibo: Father's yam

Jioma : Beautiful yam

Joachim   Biblical: God will judge

Joe : Joseph

Joel   Biblical: Jehovah is the Lord; an Old Testament prophet

Johann : A form of John Also Johannes, Johan, Jochanan

Johanna   Swahili: God's grace

John   Biblical: God is graceful, God is merciful

Johnnie : A pet form of John

Johnson   English: A surname meaning son of John

Jojo   EA: This one is a story teller

Jojo   WA: Born on Monday

Jokha   Swahili: Embroidery

Jolomi   Shekiri: The Lord has settled me

Jon : A variation of John

Jonah   Biblical: A dove; an Old Testament prophet; Jonas

Jonathan   Biblical: God has given; the son of King Saul
Jonel   A name that is probably of African-American origins
Jongilanga   SA: He faces the sun
Jordan   Biblical: To descend
Joseph   Biblical: God multiplies wealth
Josh   : A short form of Joshua
Joshua   Biblical: The Lord is my salvation
Josiah   Biblical: Fire of the Lord
Juan   Spanish form of John
Juba   Egyptian: The visitor, alsoJuber
Jubemi   Shekiri: The Lord has answered my prayers
Judd   : A form of Jordan
Jude   Biblical: Praise Prefared by Nigerian Catholics
Judhar   Swahili: Uproot
Judson   : Judah's son
Jules   : The French form of Julius
Julian   Greek: Soft-haired, light-bearded
Julio   : The Spanish form of Julian
Julius   Latin: Youthful Best known as Julius Caeser
Juma   NA: Born on Friday
Juma   NA: Born on Friday
Jumah   NA: Friday
Jumanah   Arabic: Silver pearl
Jumanne   NA: Born on Tuesday
Jumapili   Mwera: Born on Sunday
Jumba   NA: Large building
Jumoke   WA: Everyone loves the child
Justin   Latin: Justice Also Justus
Juwayria   Swahili: Rose
Juza   Swahili: Notify

K

Kacey   Irish: Brave
Kadeem   Arabic: Khadim
Kadija   WA: The porphet's wife
Kafele   WA: Worth dying for
Kafi   CA: Serene
Kafil   NA: Protector
Kagale   EA: Born in the time of trouble

Kai (Kye) Welsh: Keeper of the keys
Kai WA: Lovable
Kakra Fante: Youngest
Kakuyon CA: He arms the people
Kal : A diminutive for Kalton and Kalvin
Kalifa EA: Holy child
Kalila Arabic: Sweet heart, beloved
Kaliston Greek: (Καλιστον) Best, Beautiful
Kalolii Swahili: Feeble
Kalonji CA: He will be victorious
Kalvin : An alternate spelling for Calvin
kamali NA: Perfection
Kamania WA: Like the moon
Kamaria Swahili: One with the elegance of the moon
Kamau EA: Quiet soldier
Kamba WA: Tortoise
Kambui EA: Fearless
Kamdibe WA: Let me endure
Kame NA: Desolate
Kamil NA: Perfect
Kamilah Arabic: The perfect one
Kamilya Swahili: Perfection
Kampihe WA: God and see
Kamulira WA: Lamentable
Kamuzu WA: Medicinal
Kanavis Caribbean: Herb
Kandia WA: Fortress
Kandoro NA: A type of sweet potato
Kane Welsh: Beautiful Irish: Warrior's son
Kanika Mwera: Black
Kansiwa WA: The poor
Karama NA: Generosity
Karamoko WA: Studious
Karanja EA: A guide
Kaream : Arabic: Kareem
Kareem NA: Generous
Kareem, Karim NA: Generous
Kariamu EA: One who reflects the almighty
Karim NA: Generous
Karima Swahili: Generous

Karl : An alternate spelling of Carl
Karume EA: Protector of the land and the forest
Karume NA: Master
Kashka WA: Friendly
Kashore Swahili: Smiles
Kasimu WA: Keeper of the forest
Kasiya WA: Departure
Kassahun EA: To compensate for
Kathero EA: Born at home
Katokwe CA: Happiness is mine
Katou Uganda: Small
Kaukab Swahili: Star
Kauthar Swahili: Abundant
Kayode WA: He brought joy
Kayode Yoruba: Bring joy in
Kazandu SA: Young man
Kazija Swahili: Plenty of work
Keambirowo WA: Heap of blackness
Keane English: Of keen wit or keen eye
Keanjaho WA: Heap of beans
Keanyandaarwa WA: Heap of beans
Kedem Arabic: From the East
Kedrick Irish: A gift of splendor
Keeley Irish: Handsome Also Kealy, Keely
Keenan Irish: Little ancient one
Kefiwe Tswana: I receive grace
Kehinde Yoruba: Bring up the rear
Kehinde AA: Pet name
Kehnide WA: Twin who comes second
Keita WA: Worshipper
Keith Irish: From the battle place
Kekey Greek: (Κυριακη) Sunday Also Kiki
Kelby Scandinavian: Place by the spring
Kelechi Ibo: Praise God
Kelechi WA: Thank God
Kelinde WA: Second born of twins
Kelly Irish: Lively, aggressive
Kelsey English: One who dwells at ship island
Kelton English: Dweller in the town where ships are built
Kelvin Irish: From the narrow river Also Kelvan, Kelven

Kemba   CA: She is full of faith
Kemper   English: A variation of Kemp, which means fighter, warrior
Ken : Nickname for Kenedy, Kendall
Kendall   English: From the valley of the river Kent
Kendrick   English: Royal ruler
Kennard   English: Brave, strong
Kenneth   Irish: Handsome
Kenny : A diminutive for Kenneth
Kenyatta   EA: A musician Jomo Kenyatta, Independent movement leader
Kenyetta   EA: Sound of beautiful music
Keon   Irish: A form of John
Kermit   Irish: Free man
Kerry   Irish: Son of the dark one
Kerwin   Irish: Little black one
Kesi   EA: Born at a time when father worked hard
Kesi   NA: Judging
Ketema   EA: He comes from the valley
Keto   NA: Depth
Kevin   Irish: Handsome
Khabiri   NA: Aware
Khadejah   NA: Prophet Muhammad's first wife
Khadija, Hadija   Swahili: Prophet Muhammad's first wife
Khadijah   Arabic Name twin of prophet Muhammad's wife
Khalafu   NA: Succeed
Khalfan   NA: Successor, viceroy
Khalid   NA: Vigorous
Khalidah   Arabic: Immortal
Khalil NA: Sincere friend
Khalilah   Arabic Feminine version of Kamilah
Khalladi   NA: Lasting
Khamadi   WA: Born on Thursday
Khamis   NA:Thursday
Khamisi   NA: Born on Thursday, soldier in Prophet Muhammad's army
Khanfura   Swahili: Snort
Khari   WA: Kingly
Khary   Swahili: Khari
Khatibu   NA: Khatib orator
Khatiti   EA: Sweet little thing
Khayralla   NA: God's best
Kheri   NA: Goodness

Kheri   NA: Goodness
Khiari   NA: Preference
Khola   Swahili: Deer
Khoranhlai   WA: She who brings sun
Kiambu   EA: This one will be rich
Kiango   NA: Lampstand, light
Kibasila   NA: Insight
Kibibi   Swahili: Young lady
Kibwana   NA: Young gentleman
Kibwe   NA: Blessed
Kidawa   Swahili: Medicine
Kifimbo   Swahili: Of a fragile birth
Kifimbo   Swahili: Stick
Kigoma   NA: Small drum, joy
Kigongo   Cameroon: Born before twins
Kigongo   NA: Pole, stick, firm
Kiiza   Cameroon: Born before twins
Kijakazi   Swahili: Young maid
Kijicho   Swahili: Envious
Kilolo   CA: Youth shines on her
Kimameta   NA: Cloth
Kimani   EA: Sailor
Kimball   Irish: Bold kin
Kimweri   NA: Ruler, chief
Kinda   NA: Young bird
King   English: Ruler
Kinjeketile   Swahili: One who killed himself
Kipanja   NA: Falcon
Kirby   English: Dweller in a cottage by the water
Kirk   Scottish: Church
Kirkland   Scottish: A church's land Used as a last name
Kisasi   NA: Revenge
Kisaye   Uganda: Belonging to God
Kissa   Cameroon: Born after twins
Kit :   A nickname for Christopher
Kitunda   NA: Small fruit
Kitunzi   NA: Reward
Kizuwanda   Zaramo: The last born
Knoll   English: A round, smooth hill
Kobla   WA: Born on Tuesday

Kodjo   WA: Born on Monday
Koffi   WA: Born on Friday
Kofi   NA: Handful
Kojo   WA: Unconquerable
Kokayi   SA: Call the people to order
Kokumo   WA: This on will not die again
Kolade   Yoruba: Bring honor home
Kolawole   Yoruba: Bring honor into the house
Kolby   Polish: The dark-haired boy; a short form of Jacob
Koliraga   WA: Weeping
Kombo   NA: Impoverished, bent
Konata   WA: Man of high station
Kondo   NA: Warrior
Kongoresi   NA: Old contest
Kontar   WA: An only child
Korede   Yoruba: Harvest good things
Kotoye   Yoruba: It is important to be focused
Krishna : A Hindu god
Kufere   WA: Do not forget
Kuju   Swahili: Knowingly
Kukoyi   Yoruba: Death refused this one
Kukua   Fante: Born on Wednesday
Kunjufu   NA: Cheerful
Kunle   WA: Home is full with honors
Kurt   German: Brave and wise
Kurwa   Swahili: Repetion
Kutu   NA: One of twins
Kuumba   NA: Creativity
Kwabena   WA: Born on Tuesday
Kwacha   WA: Morning
Kwaku   WA: Born on Wednesday
Kwami   WA: Born on Saturday
Kwanza   NA: Beginning
Kwasi   WA: Born on Sunday
Kweli   NA: Truth
Kwende   WA: Let us go
Kwesi   WA: Conquering strength
Kyle   Irish: Chief

L

LaBron   French: LeBron
Lacey   Latin: From Latius's estate
Lad   English: Manservant, young man
Lagunju   Yoruba: High status sets one's face straight
Laini   Swahili: Sweet and gentle
Lali   NA: Flexible
Lamar   French: Of the sea
Lambert   German: His country's brightest
Lamia   Swahili: Glitter
Lamont   Irish: A man of the land
Lamya   Arabic: Dark-lipped
Lance   : A French diminutive for Lancelot
Landuleni   SA: One who finds greatness
Langali   SA: Sun is shining
Laraba   WA: Wednesday
Larron   French: A thief
Larry   This diminutive for Lawrence
Lars   : A Scandinavian form of Lawrence
Larvall   English: Known for a task
Lasana   CA: A poet of the people
Latham   English: A district, a division
Lathrop   English: Villager
Latif   NA: Gentle
Latifa   Swahili: Gentle
Latifah   Arabic: Gentle, kind Also Lateefah
Lavon   African-American invented
Lawanza   African: Son of the land
Lawrence   Latin: From the place of the laurel trees
Lawson   English: Son of Lawrence
Lawton   English: Settlement on a hill
Layia   WA: Born at night
Layla   EA: Born at night
Lazarus   Biblical:: God has helped
Leander   Greek: (Λεονταρι) Lion man, brave one
Leandro   Spanish: Fierce as a lion; Leandre
Lebechi   WA: Watch God
Ledell   African-American inventedcreation
Lee   English: From the pasture meadow

Leighton   English: Belonging to God Also Layton, Leyton
Lela   Swahili: Night
Lemmy : A nickname for Lemuel
Lemuel   Biblical: Belonging to God
Len   : A pet name for Leonard
Lennard : A variation of Leonard
Lennox   Irish: The land of many elm trees
Lenny : A short form of Leonard
Lenwood   English: Dweller in the tenant house in the woods
Leo   Greek: Lion
Leon   Greek: Lion
Leonard   German: Strong as a lion
Leopold   Swahili: English: A bold free man
Leroy   French: The king
Leslie   English: Dweller at the small dell
Lester   English: From Leicester
Levander   French: A man from the East
Leverett   French: Baby rabbit
Levert : Derived from the French language
Levi   Biblical: Joined, united Also Levy
Lewis   Swahili: Renowned fighter
Lex   Latin: Law
Ligongo   WA: Who is this?
Lila   Swahili: Good
Limbe   WA: Joyfulness
Lina   Arabic: Tender
Linda   SA: Goodness awaits me
Lindiwe   SA: Moment of rapture
Lindon   English: Dweller by the hill with lime trees Also Lyndon
Lindsay   English: Linden tree island
Linford   English: Dweller near the linden tree ford Also Linifred
Link   English: An enclosure
Linton : A form of Lindon
Linus   Greek: Flax-colored hair
Lionel   Latin: Young lion Also Lyonel
Lisimba   WA: Torn
Liyongo   NA: Talks nonsense
Lizwelicha   WA: New country
Ll Ghanallyn : Welsh: Ruler who is like a lion
Lloyd   Welsh: Gray-haired

Logan   Scottish: Low meadow
Lolli   Wolof: Fall
Lololi   WA: There is always love
Lolonyo   WA: Love is beautiful
Lolovivi   WA: There's always love
Lonnie : A diminutive for Alonzo
Lorenzo : The italian form of Lawrence
Lot   Biblical: To cover; the Nephew of Abraham
Lotachukwu   WA: Remember God always
Lou : A diminutive for Louis
Louis   English: Great fighter
Love : Popular in Ghana and Nigeria
Lovell   French: Young wolf
Lowell   English: Beloved
Lozokun   WA: Forget quarrel
Lubaya   Swahili: Young lioness
Lubna   Swahili: Pearl
Lubna   Kenya: Storax
Lucas : A form of Luke
Lucky : A nickname for Lucius
Luke   Greek: The giver of light
Lulu   Swahili: A pearl
Lulu   WA: Precious
Lumengo   CA: A flower of the people
Lumo   WA: Born face downwards
Lumumba   CA: Gifted, brilliant
Lumusi   Ghana: Born facedown
Lydell   English: From the wide dell
Lyle   French: One from the isle
Lyman   English: Man of the meadows
Lymore : An unusual given name of obscure origins
Lyndall   English: From the lime tree dell
Lyron   French: The lyrical one
Lysander   Greek: (Λυσανδρος) He liberates
Lyutha   Swahili: The wealthy

M

Maabade   NA: Sanctuary
Maalik   NA: King, qwner

Maamuni   NA: Reliable

Maanan   Akan: Fourth born child

Maarifa   NA: Experience

Maasuma   Swahili: Inpeccable

Mablevi   WA: Don't deceive

Mabruke   NA: Blessed

MacArthur   Irish: Son of Arthur

Macdonald   Scottish: Son of Donald

Maceo   Spanish: From Matthew's estate

Machano   NA: Born on Wednesday

Macharia   EA: An eternal friend

Machui   Swahili: Leopord like

Machumu   EA: Blacksmith

Machungwa   NA: Orange season

Machupa   WA: One who likes to drink

Mack   : A pet form of Mac rarely used as a given name

Mackinley   Irish: Son of the learned or skilled one

Maclean   English: Son of Leander

Madaadi   WA: An age group

Madhubuti   NA: Steadfast

Madiha   Swahili: Praiseworthy

Madihah   Arabic: Praiseworthy

Madison   English: Son of a mighty warrior

Madu   WA: Man

Maduabuchi   Ibo: Human beings are not anybody's God

Maduabuchi   WA: Man is not God

Maduabueke   Ibo: Human beoings are not the Creator

Maduakomba   Ibo: A town cannot be short of people

Maduamuwa   Ibo: Men do not understand the world

Madubuchi   Ibo: One may make or unmake another

Madubuego   Ibo: Human beings render services which money provides

Madubuife   Ibo: Human beings are valuable

Madubuike   Ibo: The possession of human beings is a source of power

Madubuine   Ibo: One can take pride in the possession of human beings

Madubuko   Ibo: Human being constitute the source of quarrel

Maduegbum   Ibo: People will not kill me

Maduekeibe   Ibo: Man does not create his fellows

Maduekwenjo   Ibo: Men should not consent to evil

Maduemeka   Ibo: People have done very well

Maduemekata   Ibo: People did so much

Maduemezie   Ibo: People have done well

Madukaego   Ibo: A human being is more important tha money

Madukaife   Ibo: Human beings are more valuable than eve

Madukaku   Ibo: Human beings are more important than wealth

Madzimoyo   WA: Water of life

Mae, Maryam,   Swahili: Mary

Mafaune   Bachopi: Soil

Magano   SA: Gift

Magoma   NA: Celebration

Maha   NA: Beautiful eyes

Mahbuba   Swahili: Beloved

Mahbuub   NA: Beloved

Mahdi   NA: Rightfully guided

Mahfuda   Swahili: Protected

Mahfuudh   NA: Preserved

Mahluli   SA: Victory

Mahluli   WA: Victor

Mahmud   NA: Praised

Maidei   WA: What did you want?

Maideyi   SA: What did you expect

Maisha   Swahili: Life

Maizah   Arabic: Discerning rains

Majaliwa   NA: Destined

Majid   Swahili: Maajid innovator

Majidah   Arabic: Glorious

Major   Latin: Greater

Majuto   NA: Regret

Maka   Swahili: Mecca

Makame   NA: High rank, ruler

Makamu   NA: Dignified

Makinde   Yoruba: Bring home the valiant man

Makinwa   Yoruba: Bring the valiant man

Makonnen   EA: Ruler

Makungu   NA: Initiation

Makutano   WA: Born in a meeting place

Makwetu   Swahili: Our place

Malachi   Biblical: Messenger of God

Malaika   Swahili: Angel

Malak   Arabic: Angel

Malaki   Swahili: Angel

Malawa   WA: Flowers
Malcolm   Scottish: A disciple of St Columba
Malek   NA: Owner
Malene   WA: Tower
Maliaka   Swahili: Queen Also Malaika
Maliha   Swahili: Pleasant
Maliik   NA: King, also Maliki
Malik   NA: Owner
Malik   NA: King; Maliki
Malikia   Swahili: Queen
Mallory   German: Army counselor
Malvern   Welsh: Bare hill
Mama   Fante: Born on Saturday
Mambo   NA: Matters, events
Mamboleo   WA: Temporary
Mamoun   NA: Confident
Manabaraka   Swahili: Brings blessings
Mandara   NA: Leader
Mande   Uganda: First day
Mandisa   Xhosa: Sweet
Maneno   NA: Words
Manfred   German: Man of peace
Manga   Swahili: Emigrant
Mangwiro   SA: The enlightened one
Mani   CA: He came from the mountain
Manley   English: Dweller at the hero's meadow
Manning   English: Son of the hero
Manny   English: nickname for Emanuel
Mansa   Akan: Third born child
Mansfield   English: Dweller in the field by the small river
Mansuur   NA: Protected
Manu   Hindu: A mythical creator of humankind
Manuel   Spanish: God is with us; a form of Emmanuel
Manus   Irish: Great king
Manville   French: He comes from the great estate
Manzi   NA: Residence
Mapfumo   SA: The soildier
Mapute   NA: Empty, taken away
Maram   Arabic: Aspiration
Marcel   : The French form of Marcellus

Marcellus   Latin: Little warlike one
Marcus   Latin: Little hammer, warlike one
Mariama   WA: Gift of God
Marifa   Swahili: Experience
Mario : An Italian form of Mark
Marion : This French masculine form of Mary
Marjani   Swahili: Coral
Marjani   Swahili: Named for the beautiful coral
Mark   Latin: From Mars, the Roman god of war
Marka   WA: Steady rain
Marland   English: From the land of the lake
Marley   Irish: One who lives near the lake meadow
Marlon   French: Blackbird Also Marlin
Mars   Latin: The god of war
Marshall   English: Military cavalry officer
Martin   English: Warrior
Martinez : The Spanish form of Martin
Marty : A nickname for Martin
Marvin   English: Well-known friend
Marzuku   NA: Blessed
Masamba   WA: Leaves
Masani   Cameroon: Has gap between teeth
Masani   WA: Has gap between teeth
Masara   Swahili: Happiness
Mash'al   NA: Torch
Mashama   SA: A surprise
Mashavu   Swahili: Cheeks
Masibuwa   WA: Modern days
Masika Swahili: Born during the season
Masika   Kenya: Rainy season
Masika   WA: Born during rainy season
Maskini   Swahili: Humble
Maskini   WA: Poor
Mason   French: A worker in stone Popular last name in the Caribbean
Mastura   Swahili: Protected
Masud   NA: Fortunate
Matari   NA: Rainy season
Mathis : A form of Mattew
Mathna   Swahili: Praise
Matima   Swahili: Full moon

Matogo   NA: Markings on the face
Matsimela   SA: The roots are firm
Matthew   Biblical: Gift of god
Matuka   Swahili: Emancipated
Matumbo   Swahili: The honored one
Matunde   WA: Fruits
Matwa   NA: Sensible
Maua   Swahili: Flowers
Maudisa   WA: Sweet
Maulana   NA: Our master
Maulidi   EA: Born during the month of Maulidi
Maurice   Latin: The dark-skinned one
Maury   : A nickname for Maurice
Mavro   Greek: Black
Mawakana   CA: I yield to the ancestors
Mawali   WA: There is a God
Mawasi   WA: In God's hands
Mawulode   WA: God will provide
Mawulolo   WA: God is great
Mawusi   Ghana: In the hands of God
Maxwell   English: From Mack's well
Mayasa   Swahili: Walks proudly
Mayfield   English: From the warrior's field
Mayhew   : The French form of Matthew
Mayinuna   WA: Expressive
Maymuna   Swahili: Blessed
Maynard   French: Powerful
Maysara   Swahili: Ease
Mbaarak   NA: Blessed
Mbachuobia   Ibo: Pople do not turn out their guest
Mbadiegwu   Ibo: People are bizarre
Mbaenyi   Ibo: Powerful tribe
Mbafor   Ibo: Home of major market place
Mbagun   NA: One of twins
Mbakogu   Ibo: More of words than action
Mbakwebia   Ibo: People will come upon consent
Mbamba   NA: Branch of a tree, thin
Mbaonu   Ibo: Boastful mouth
Mbaya   NA: Bad, ugly
Mbeke   Ibo: Born on the third market day

Mbita   NA: Quiet
Mbiyu   EA: This one runs fast
Mbkondja   SA: My struggles
Mbogo   NA: Buffalo, spokesman
Mbonisi   SA: Teacher
Mboza   Swahili: A type of tree
Mbwana   NA: Master
Mbwana   WA: Master
Mchawi   NA: Magician
Mdahoma   NA: Long life
Mdogo   NA: Young
Mead   English: From the meadow
Mebude   Yoruba: Bring a gift home
Medgar   : Name of the slain civil rights leader
Mel   : A diminutive for names such as Melvin
Melvin   Irish: Chief
Mema   Swahili: Goodness
Menana   WA: Lustrous
Menkaliya   Swahili: From Mmenikaliya area
Mensa   WA: Third Son
Mercer   English: Merchant or storekeeper
Merrill   French: Little famous one
Merritt   English: Worthy
Mertin   English: From the town by the sea Also Merton
Mervyn   Welsh: Sea hill Also Mervin
Meyer   French: The bearer of light
Meyyaan   Swahili: Not a real friend
Mfaki   NA: Exalted
Mfaume   NA: King
Mganga   EA: A doctor
Mgbafo   Ibo: On the day of afo
Mgbafor   WA: Born on Afor market day
Mgbechi   Ibo: God's time
Mgbeke   Ibo: On the day of Eke (A female born on Eke day)
Mgbeke   WA: Born on Eke market day
Mgbeorie   Ibo: A female born on Orie (market day) day
Mgeni   NA: Visitor
Mgeni   Swahili: Visitor
Mhina   NA: Comfort
Micere   EA: Has a strong will

Michael   Biblical: He who is like God
Mickey : A pet name for Michae
Migozo   CA: She is ernest
Miguel   The Spanish form of Michael
Mijiza   EA: Works with her hands
Mike : A popular diminutive for Michael
Mila   Swahili: Traditions
Miles   English: Merciful Also Myles
Milford   English: A place name meaning from the ford near the mill
Milt : A popular diminutive for Milton
Milton   English: Dwells in the town near the mill
Miriam   Swahili: I am
Mirza   NA: Prince
Mitch : A diminutive for Mitchell
Mitchell   English: A form of Michael
Miujiza   NA: Miracle
Mkadam   NA: Ahead, leader
Mkali   Swahili: Fierce
Mkamba   NA: Rope maker
Mkiwa   Swahili: Orphaned
Mkiyoni   Swahili: From Hamkiyoni
Mkubwa   NA: Senior
Mkweli   Swahili: Truthful
Mmabuiro   Ibo: Beauty breeds enemies
Mmaku   Ibo: Beauty of wealth
Mmanga   Swahili: A trip
Modeira   WA: Teacher
Modibo   WA: Helper
Modupe   WA: I'm greatful
Modupe   Yoruba: I am grateful
Mogbeyi   Shekiri: This one is my joy
Mohammed   NA: Thankful
Molefi   SA: Preserver of tradition
Momar   SA: This one is a philosopher
Mombera   EA: He loves adventure
Mona   NA: A great surprise
Mongo   WA: Famous
Monifa   Yoruba: I have luck
Monroe   Irish: Dweller at the river's mouth
Montgomery   French: From the wealth one's hill castle

Monti : A nickname for Montgomery
Montsho Tswana: Black
Moore French: A dark handsome man; from the moors
Morgan Welsh: He dwells by the white sea
Moriba WA: Curious
Morrell English: Dark-complexioned one
Morris Latin: Dark-skinned
Morrison English: Son of Maurice
Moses Biblical: Taken out of the water
Mosi EA: She is the first born
Mosi Swahili: The first born
Mosi WA: First born
Mouna NA: Little moon Also Mouni
Moyo WA: God health
Moza Swahili: Distinguished
Mozell : This name is uniquely African-American
Mpasa WA: A local Mat
Mpho Tswana: Gift
Mpumelelo WA: Success
Mpyama CA: He shall inherit
Mrashi Swahili: Rose water sorinkler
Mrehe NA: East life
Msamaki NA: Fisherman
Msellem NA: Flawless
Mshabaha NA: Resemblance
Mshangama NA: Rising
Mshinda Swahili: Successful
Msiba Swahili: Born during mourning
Mtakuja Swahili: You will come
Mtama Swahili: Millet
Mtavila NA: You'll must swallow it
Mtembezi NA: One who roams about
Mtheto SA: One who loves the law of the land
Mthinklulu SA: Strong as a tree
Mtoro NA: Runaway
Mtumwa Swahili: Messenger
Mtunzi SA: This one is thunderous
Muata SA: One who searchs for the truth
Mubaadar NA: Undertakes
Muchaneta SA: Perhaps you will be fatigued

Mudiwa   SA: Truly loved
Mudiwa   WA: Beloved
Mudiwa   Shona: Beloved
Mudrik   NA: Intelligent
Mufid   NA: Beneficial
Mufiida   Swahili: Beneficial
Muga   EA: Mother of all
Mugabe   CA: Intelligent, quick
Mugeta   EA: One born at night
Mugo   EA: A wise person
Muhamadi, Muhammed   NA : Praised, commendable
Muhammad   NA: Commendable
Muhashsham   NA: Respected
Muhidini   NA: Revivalist
Muhima   Swahili: Important
Muhsin   NA: Beneficent
Muhyiddin   NA: Bestower of religion
Mukamtagara   WA: Born in the time of war
Mukamutara   WA: Mutara's daughter
Mukamutaro   WA: Mutara's son
Mukhtaar   NA: Chosen
Mukumtagara   EA: Born at war time
Mukumutara   EA: Born during Mutara
Mulekwa   Uganda: Child born out of wedlock
Mumbejja   Uganda: Princess
Muna   Swahili: Hope
Muna   Arabic: Wish
Mundhir   NA: Sign, reminder
Muniir   NA: Shining
Munim   NA: Benefactor
Munira   Swahili: Radiant
Muobuife   Ibo: The spirit world is real
Muodi   Ibo: Beware of the evil
Muoegbum   Ibo: The spirit will not kill me
Muoha   Ibo: The People's wish
Muokweadi   Ibo: If the spirit approves we will survive
Muokwougo   Ibo: May the spirit give reward
Muolokwu   Ibo: May the spirit decide
Muomaife   Ibo: Spirits cannot be deceived
Muomaoke   Ibo: The spirits know our limitations

Muombwa   NA: Beseeched
Muonwendu   Ibo: The gods preserve life
Muonweuche   Ibo: The spirits are wise
Muonwike   Ibo: Strength belongs to the spirits
Muraad   NA: Good intention
Murphy   Irish: Sea warrior
Murray   Irish: Warrior who dwells by the sea
Murshid   NA: Guide
Murtadha   NA: Disciplined
Musa moses   NA: Powerful
Musa   NA: Moses
Musa   NA: Sharp
Muslih   NA: Reformer
Muslim   NA: Submits to God peacefully
Mustafa   NA: Chosen one
Mustafa   NA: Well chosen
Muteteli   Rwanda: Dainty
Mutope   CA: Protector
Muumin   NA: Believer
Muyaka   NA: Truthful
Muyiwa   Yoruba: Brought this one
Muzaana   Uganda: The wife of a princess
Mvita   Swahili: Full of life
Mwa   WA: Beauty
Mwai   WA: Good fortune
Mwajuma   Swahili: born on Friday
Mwaka   Swahili: Born in new year
Mwaka   Ibo: A child is the best blessing
Mwalimu   NA: Teacher
Mwamini   Swahili: Believer
Mwammoja   Swahili: First one
Mwana   Swahili: Lady
Mwanadongo   Swahili: Child of the land
Mwanahamisi   Swahili: Born on Thursday
Mwanahawa   Swahili: Mother of humankind
Mwanaidi   Swahili: Born on Muslim Holy day
Mwanakhamisi   Swahili: Born on Thursday
Mwanakheri   Swahili: Brings goodness
Mwanakweli   Swahili: Brings trut
Mwanamize   Swahili: Distinguished

Mwando   EA: An efficient worker
Mwanga   NA: Light
Mwangi   EA: He will have many children
Mwanjaa   Zaramo: Born during a feminine
Mwanze   CA: The child is protected
Mwapacha   NA: Twin
Mwari a   Swahili: Girl who has reached puberty
Mwasaa   NA: Born on time
Mwasaa   Swahili: Timely
Mwasham   Swahili: Unlucky
Mwata   CA: We have been sensible
Mwatabu   Swahili: Person of difficulty
Mwema   Swahili: Good
Mwendapole   NA: Walks cautiously
Mwinyi   NA: Ruler
Mwinyimadi   NA: Just ruler
Mwinyimkuu   NA: Great ruler
Mwita   WA: The caller
Mxali   SA: Anxiety is over
Mxolisi   SA: Peacemaker
Myron   Greek: (Μυρωδια) Fragrant, sweet oil
Mzale   NA: Native
Mzee   NA: Elderly

N

N'namdi   WA: Worthy
Naadir   NA: Rare
Naadu   Ga: One from the Sempeh region
Naaman   Biblical: Honorable, good pleasant, beautiful
Naasa   Swahili: Skillful
Naasir   NA: Defender
Nabate   WA: Little
Nabhani   NA: Sensible, judicious
Nabil   NA: Noble
Nabila   Swahili: Noble
Nabinye   WA: Producer of twins
Nabirye   Cameroon: Mother
Nabulungi   Cameroon: Beautiful one

Nabulungg   WA: Beautiful one
Nabwire   Uganda: Born during the night
Nada   Arabic: Full of generosity
Nadhari   Swahili: Vision
Nadhim   NA: Organizer
Nadhira   Swahili: Foremost
Nadia   NA: Time of promise
Nadia   Swahili: Caller
Nadif   EA: Born between two seasons
Nadif   WA: Born between the two seasons
Nadifa   EA: Born between seasons
Nadir   NA: Rare
Nadiya   Swahili: Generous
Nadra   Swahili: Scarce
Naeemah   Arabic: Benevolent
Nafisa   Mali: Precious
Nafisa   Swahili: Priceless gem
Nafisah   Arabic: Precious
Nafla   Swahili: Gift
Nafula   WA: Born during rainy season
Nafuma   WA: Born feet first
Nailah   Arabic: She who will succeed
Naima   Swahili: Graceful
Najaat   Swahili: Safety
Najah   Swahili: Success
Najat   NA: Safe
Najibah   Arabic: Of noble birth
Najiib   NA: Noble
Najla   Swahili: Progeny
Najla   Arabic: Wide eyes
Najma   Swahili: Star
Najuma   EA: She abounds in joy
Najya   Swahili: Saved
Nakampi   Uganda: Short
Nakisisa   WA: Child of the shadows
Nakpangi   CA: This one is a star
Naliaka   WA: Wedding
Nalo   WA: Much loved
Nalongo   Cameroon: This is a mother of twins
Nalongo   WA: Mothers of twins

Namalwa   Uganda: Born of twins
Namono   WA: Younger of twins
Nana   WA: Mother of the earth
Nangleni   WA: Fish
Nanji   NA: Safe
Nantambu   WA: Man of destiny
Nanyamka   Ghana: God's gift
Nargisi   Swahili: Narcissus
Nasiche   Uganda: Born during the time of locust
Nasiim   Swahili: Fresh air
Nasiir   NA: Helper
Nasike   WA: Born in the locust season
Nasila   NA: Honey
Nasor   NA: Saved
Nasra   Swahili: Assistance
Nassor   WA: Victorious
Nat   : For Nathan or Nathaniel
Nataki   CA: She is of royal birth
Natasha   Swahili: Variant of Natalia
Nathan   Biblical: Messenger
Nathaniel   Biblical: A gift of God
Nathari   NA: Embroidery
Nathifa   Arabic: Clean
Nayfa   Swahili: Benefit
Nayla   Swahili: Gain
Nayo   Yoruba: We have joy
Naysun   Swahili: Dangling seedless grapes
Nazim   NA: Wonderful
Ndale   WA: Trick
Ndapewa   SA: This belongs to me
Ndidi   Ibo: Patience
Ndidikanma   Ibo: Patience is the best
Ndoro   SA: The emblem of kingship
Ndubia   Ibo: May life become bountiful
Ndubuaku   Ibo: Life is wealth
Ndubueze   Ibo: Life is incomparable
Ndubuisi   Ibo: Life is valuable
Ndubuka   Ibo: Trouble cannot be avoided by a living being
Ndubumma   Ibo: There is no beauty without life
Ndudi   Ibo: If there is life

Ndudimma   Ibo: Life is good
Ndudinkpa   Ibo: Life is important
Nduefuefu   Ibo: Life never seizes
Nduejuafo   Ibo: One is never tired of living
Ndueze   Ibo: Life of the king
Nduka   WA: Life is supreme
Ndukaku   Ibo: Life is more important than wealth
Ndukwe   WA: If life permits
Ndulu   WA: Dove
Ndumiso   SA: Praise follows this one
Ndunda   CA: We are happy
Ndunga   CA: She will be famous
Neal   Irish: Chief, champion Also Neil
Ned   : This diminutive for Edward or Edmond implies wealth
Neema   Swahili: Born during prosperous times
Neimat   NA: Pleasant
Nelson   Irish: Son of Neal Nelson Mandela, President of SA
Nena   Swahili: Speak
Nero   Latin: Strong, stern
Nestor   Greek: Wise elder
Ngachi   Ibo: The place for chi
Ngadiuba   Ibo: Where there are homes for many
Ngboro   Efik: Lady of strength
Ngena   EA: Majestic in service
Ngicuro   EA: Born in the plains
Ngimonia   EA: People of the forest
Ngina   EA: One who serves
Ngoli   WA: Happiness
Ngozi   Ibo: Blessing
Ngozichuku   Ibo: God's blessing
Ngozikike   Ibo: Blessing is more valuable than power
Ngugi   EA: The traditions are set
Ngulinga   Ogoni: Weeping
Ngunda   WA: Dove
Nguvumali   NA: Power is wealth
Nia   Swahili: Purpose
Niambi   CA: The melody is heard
Niamoja   NA: One purpose
Nianmke   WA: God's gift
Niara   Swahili: Of high purpose

Nicholas   Greek: (Νικω) The victorious one; Nichols, Nickolas, Nickolaus
Nick Nickname for Nicholas; Nicky, Nickey (not used indepedently)
Nigel   Irish: Champion
Nijideka   WA: Survival is paramount
Niles   African: A river in Egypt
Niles   English: Son of Neal Also Nyles
Nilotes   EA: Born at the river Niger
Nimrod   Biblical: Rebel Found in the 19th century
Nina   Swahili: Mother
Nini   WA: Strong
Nisriin   Swahili: Wild rose
Nisrim   Swahili: Wild rose
Njabulo   SA: Happiness
Njansi   Ibo: A poisonous place
Njemile   Yao: Upstanding
Njeri   EA: Daughter of a warrior
Njonjo   EA: Disciplined
Nkachukwu   Ibo: God's skill
Nkakwaonwu   Ibo: Death cannot be prevented by human skill
Nkandinshuti   WA: I like friends
 Nkechi   Ibo: Belongs to God
Nkechinyere   WA: Whichever God gives
Nkeka   WA: Tenderness
Nkemdiche   Ibo: I am special
Nkemdirim   WA: Let mine be with me
Nkemefula   WA: Let me not lose mine
Nkenge   CA: She is brilliant
Nkokheli   SA: He is a leader
Nkosi   SA: He will rule
Nkpume   WA: Solid as rock
Nkroma   Akan: The ninth child
Nkruma   WA: Ninth born
Nkululeko   SA: Freedom is ours
Nkwodimma   Ibo: Nkwo market day is favorable to me
Nmabuugwu   Ibo: Beauty has prestige
Nnabuchi   Ibo: A Father is a child's chi
Nnabude   Ibo: It is the father that makes the child famous
Nnabudo   Ibo: Father is the source of peace
Nnabugwu   WA: Father is honor
Nnabuihe   Ibo: A father is a valuable asset

Nnabuihem   WA: Father is worth a lot
Nnabuike   Ibo: Father is strength
Nnabuisi   Ibo: Life comes first
Nnabuugwu   Ibo: Father is source of child's honor
Nnachem   Ibo: May father protect me
Nnadi   Ibo: The father of one's husband
Nnadiekwe   Ibo: One yields if father is alive
Nnadiugwu   Ibo: The presence of a father is pretigeous
Nnaemeka   WA: Father has done much
Nnaji   Ibo: Father of yams
Nnajiofo   Ibo: Father is in the path of righteousness
Nnaku   Ibo: The wealthy father
Nnamala   Ibo: Father knows the traditions of the land/people
Nnamdi   WA: My father is alive
Nnamuche   Ibo: Father understands people's intentions
Nnanna   Ibo: Father's father
Nnanne   Ibo: Nnanneya, Nnennaya Mother's father (Short form: Ne)
Nnanwenwa   Ibo: Father owns the child
Nne   WA: Mother
Nnebuisi   Ibo: Nothing is more important than mother
Nnedimma   Ibo: Mother is good to have
Nnediugwu   Ibo: Mother is the source of prestige
Nnediuto   Ibo: Mother is a pleasure to have
Nneka   Ibo: Amother is the greatest
Nnekamkpa   Ibo: Mothers are very valuable
Nnenna   Ibo: Father's mother
Nnennaya   WA: Her father's mother
Nnenne   Ibo: Mother's mother
Nnenwekele   Ibo: Thanks are due to mothers
Noah   Biblical: Rest, peace, long-lived
Noah   NA: Consolation
Nobantu   SA: Beloved by all
Nobanzi   Xhosa: Width
Nobini   SA: Blessed with two girls
Noble   Latin: An aristocrat
Nobuhle   WA: Beauty
Nocawe   SA: She was born on Sunday
Noel   French: Christmas
Nogomo   CA: He will be prosperous

Nokhwezi   SA: A morning star
Nolizwe   WA: County
Nomabaso   SA: A welcome present
Nomatha   SA: A real surprise
Nombeko   Xhosa: Respect
Nombese   WA: A wonderful child
Nomble   Xhosa: Beautiful
Nombulelo   SA: I give thanks
Nompumelelo   SA: Kindness is found
Nomthandazo   SA: We prayed to the ancestors
Nomusa   SA: This is mercy
Nomuula   Xhosa: Rain
Nondudumo   SA: The time was thunderous
Noni   WA: Gift of God
Nonkulueko   SA: Freedom is here
Nontando   SA: Full of love
Nontiupheko   SA: end of suffering
Nontobeko   SA: Humility is approaching
Nontothuzelo   SA: She will console us
Nonyameko   Xhosa: Patience
Nonyelum   WA: Abide with me
Nonzenzele   SA: She is capable
Nonzwakazi   SA: This is elegance
Norman   English: Man of the Northern Region
Norris   Scottish: One from the Northern Region
Norton   English: Dweller in the Northern town
Norvell   English: From the Northern estate
Nosakhene   WA: God's way is the only way
Nosiike   WA: Be firm
Noxolo   SA: Peaceful
Nozibele   SA: She is generous
Nozipho   SA: A gift
Nsobundu   Ibo: To follow traditon is life itself
Nsombi   CA: Abounding joy
Nsonwa   Akan: The seventh child
Ntathu   SA: I have three girls
Ntombentle   SA: A lovely girl
Ntombizine   SA: The fourth girl
Ntombizodwa   SA: All are girls
Ntosake   Zulu: She who walks with lions; Ntozake

Ntsikelelo SA: Blessing
Nuebese Benin: A wonderful child
Nuha Swahili: Consoled
Nulungo CA: She is beautiful
Nun NA: Brightness
Nunu Swahili: Extol
Nura Swahili: Brightness
Nuru Swahili: Born in daylight
Nuuh NA: Noah, consoled
Nuzha Swahili: Pleasure
Nwabatanobi Ibo: May children be endeared
Nwabuaku Ibo: A child is wealth
Nwabuanuli Ibo: A child is the source of joy
Nwabude Ibo: A child is a person's source of fame
Nwabudike WA: Child is power
Nwabudo Ibo: A child brings peace in the home
Nwabueze Ibo: It is child that gives the parents the highest status
Nwabugo Ibo: A child is the source of one's glory
Nwabugwu Ibo: A child is a source of respect
Nwabuibe Ibo: A child is like his fellow children
Nwabuigwo A child id the price we pay
Nwabuihe Ibo: A child is valuable
Nwabuike Ibo: A child is the source of strength
Nwabuikwu Ibo: It is children that make relations
Nwabuisi Ibo: The possession of a child is the first priority
Nwabuko Ibo: A child is the source of pride
Nwabulo Ibo: To have a child is to have a home
Nwabumbu Ibo: The possesssion of a child is a priority
Nwabundo Ibo: A child is the source of rest and protection
Nwabundozi WA: A child is a Ibo: blessing
Nwabundu Ibo: Life is empty without a child
Nwabungozi Ibo: A child is a source of/constitutes blessing
Nwabunike Ibo: A child cannot be acquired by force or strength
Nwabuogo Ibo: A child comes only as a favor
Nwabuoku Ibo: A child is a source of wealth
Nwabuonu Ibo: A possession of a child can make one boastful
Nwabuonyiye Ibo: A child comes only as a gift from God
Nwabuwa Ibo: The world/life is worthless without a child
Nwabuzo Ibo: A child opens endless avenues in life
Nwachi Ibo: Child of God

Nwachukwu   Ibo: Child of God
Nwadi   Ibo: A valuable child exists
Nwadiaguu   Ibo: One thirsts for a child
Nwadialu   Ibo: The training of a child is a heavy duty
Nwadighu   Ibo: A child is a thing of beauty
Nwadike   Ibo: a child is hard to come by
Nwadimkpa   Ibo: A child is important
Nwadimkpa   Ibo: A child is important
Nwadimma   Ibo: A child is good
Nwadinobi   Ibo: A child is dear
Nwadinso   Ibo: A child is innocent
Nwadiogo   Ibo: A child is a thing of beauty
Nwadiuko   Ibo: A child is hard to come by
Nwadiuko   Ibo: A child is scarce
Nwadiuto   Ibo: A chil dis delightful to have
Nwadum   Ibo: May child lead me to the end
Nwaeda   Ibo: A daughter to the family
Nwaego   Ibo: Child of wealth
Nwaeke   Ibo: Child born on eke market day
Nwafo   Ibo: Child born on afo market day
Nwagbara   Ibo: Child of spirit beings
Nwagbogu   Ibo: May a child bring an end to the quarrel
Nwagboso   WA: A child does not run
Nwagha   Ibo: Child born during the war
Nwaigwe   Ibo: A child of the firmament
Nwaiwu   Ibo: Child of law
Nwajagu   Ibo: Child of the wildness
Nwajianuri   Ibo: Happiness is brought by a child
Nwajindu   Ibo: A child owns life
Nwakaegbo   Ibo: A child is more valuable than money
Nwakaji   Ibo: A child is more valuable than the possesion of a yam
Nwakanma   Ibo: Child is better than every thing else
Nwakego   Ibo: A child is outstanding
Nwakoako   Ibo: Children are never lacked
Nwakoulo   Ibo: A home is never without a child
Nwakuba   Ibo: A child is more valuable than wealth
Nwamaife   Ibo: Children are intelligent
Nwamaife   WA: An intelligent child
Nwamaka   Ibo: A child is so beautiful
Nwamanna   Ibo: The child does not know his father

Nwamara   Ibo: Child of grace
Nwamma   Ibo: A child of beauty
Nwamuo   Ibo: Child of the spirits
Nwandu   Ibo: Child of life
Nwangene   Ibo: Child of the stream
Nwanjideknma   Ibo: It pays to be self reliant
Nwankwo   Ibo: Child born on Nkwo market day
Nwanne   Ibo: Mother's child
Nwanneka   Ibo: Brotherhood is better
Nwannekauto   Ibo: Children of the same mother are very valuable
Nwanodu   WA: May the child survive
Nwanwa   Ibo: Grand child
Nwanyibuaku   Ibo: A female child is a source of wealth
Nwanyibuihe   Ibo: The female sex are valuable
Nwanyibunwa   Ibo: A female is good a child as the male
Nwanyimma   Ibo: Woman of beauty
Nwanyiocha   Ibo: Fair complexioned woman
Nwanyioma   Ibo: A beautiful lady
Nwanyiudo   Ibo: Woman of peace
Nwanyiugbo   Ibo: A woman from abroad, outside
Nwaobere   Ibo: A litle child
Nwaobi   Ibo: Child from esteemed compound
Nwaogo   Ibo: A child of the gods
Nwaoha   Ibo: Child of the people
Nwaoji   Ibo: A child of strength
Nwaola   Ibo: Beautiful child of grace
Nwaoma   Ibo: Beautiful child
Nwaorie   Ibo: A child born on Orie market day
Nwosu   Ibo: A sacred child
Nwaozuzu   Ibo: A child of perfection
Nwaudo   Ibo: A child of peace
Nwaugo   Ibo: Child of elegance
Nwogu   Ibo: Child of righteousness
Nwokedi   Ibo: There is no shortage of the manly folk
Nwokedinma   Ibo: A male child is valuable/desirable
Nwokenta   Ibo: A male small in size
Nwokeoma   Ibo: Handsome man
Nwokeudo   Ibo: Man of peace
Nwokocha   Ibo: Fair complexioned man
Nwuche   Ibo: Thought provoking child

Nwugo   Ibo: Like eagle
Nyahkomago   WA: Second child after twin
Nyameke   Akan: Gift from God
Nyandoro   SA: He wears the crown
Nyathuma   CA: A helper of others
Nyemba   WA: Beans
Nyenyedzi   SA: Star
Nyikadzino   SA: This land belongs to us
Nyimbo   Swahili: Song
Nyiramohoro   WA: Peaceful
Nyuni   NA: Bird
Nzeadiujo   Ibo: Titled man is courageous
Nzebuihe   Ibo: Nze is more imporatant in the society
Nzenwuka   Ibo: Speech is reserved to the rulers
Nzezom   Ibo: May my mother defend me
Nzinga   CA: She is beauty and courageous

O

Oakley   English: From the field of oak trees Used as a last name
Oare   WA: Saintly
Oba   WA: King
Obadele   WA: The king comes home
Obadiah   Swahili: Servant of God
Obafemi   WA: The king likes me
Obaji   Ibo: A barn for yams
Obaseki   WA: The Oba surpasses the market
Obasiukwu   Calabar: Great God
Obiaeri   Ibo: One who comes to enjoy wealth
Obiagaeliaku   Benin: She has come to enjoy
Obiajulu   WA: The heart is consoled
Obiajunwa   Ibo: The heart cannot reject children
Obiajunwa   WA: The heart does not reject
Obiaku   Ibo: A family of wealth
Obialo   WA: The heart is conforted
Obiamaiwe   Ibo: The heart that knows no anger
Obiamamba   Ibo: A person that does not know the order of things
Obianuju   Benin: Born at the time of plenty
Obianuria   WA: The heart is happy

Obiatuegwu   Ibo: The heart does not fear

Obibuaku   Ibo: To be rich in kindred is to be wealthy

Obichukwu   Ibo: God's will

Obidiegwu   : The heart is wonderful

Obidike   Ibo: The heart of the valiant

Obidiya   Ibo: The heart of a husband

Obiefuefu   Ibo: The lineage will not continue

Obiego   Ibo: The desire for money

Obileye   Yoruba: Parents have dignity and respect

Obinna   Ibo: The wish of the father

Obinna   WA: Heart of the father

Obinne   Ibo: Heart of the mother

Obinwa   Ibo: A heart that throbs for a child

Obinwanne   Ibo: The heart of brotherhood

Obinwoke   Ibo: The heart; courageous heart of a man

Obiocha   Ibo: Pure heart

Obioma   Ibo: Kindhearted

Obiukwu   Ibo: Great compound

Oboego   Ibo: The child that came with money

Oboi   EA: The second son

Obuchionye   Ibo: Whose God is he?

Obueke   Ibo: Is he the Creator?

Ochi   WA: Laughter

Ochieng   WA: Born during the daytime

Ochiobi   Ibo: The hidden laugh

Ochiogu   Ibo: Leader of war

Ochiulo   Ibo: Thelaugh at home

Ochuba   Ibo: The seeker of wealth

Ochubuiro   Ibo: Murder brings about enmity

Odai   EA: The third son

Ode   Benin: Born along the road

Odebunmi   Yoruba: Hunter gave me

Odedairo   Yoruba: Brave hunter

Odell   Scandinavian: Wealthy one

Odibochukwu   Ibo: The servant of God

Odiche   Ibo: Is it different?

Odie   : A diminutive for Odell; Odey

Odiegwu   Ibo: Is it wonderful?

Odinakachukwu   WA: In God's hands

Oding   EA: An artist

Odinkemere   WA: Have I done anything?

Odion   WA: The first of twins

Odionu   Ibo: Is it not dumbfounding?

Odoyoye   Yoruba: Oracular utterance rejoices at a title

Oduagu   Ibo: The tail of a leopard

Oduenyi   Ibo: The tail of an elephant

Odufunnade   Yoruba: Oracle gave me a crown

Oduguwa   Yoruba: Oracular utterance straightens character

Oduji   Ibo: The tender and valuable

Odunewu   Yoruba: A dangerous year

Oduneye   Yoruba: Diviners have diginity

Odunlami   Yoruba: Festivals have distinctive marks

Odunmbaku   Yoruba: The year I would have died

Oduntan   Yoruba: A year of a story

Oduoha   Ibo: The leader of the people

Oduola   Yoruba: Honor

Odusanwo   Yoruba: Oracular utterance pays money

Odusanya   Yoruba: Oracule compensates for suffering

Odutola   Yoruba: Oracular utterance is sufficient to confer status

Ofobuike   Ibo: TO be upright is to have moral strength

Ofobuju   Ibo: To be upright id to bein plenty

Ofobundu   Ibo: Uprightness is the essence of life

Ofodire   Ibo: Truthfullness is effective

Ofoegbum   : Ofo will not kill me

Ofon   Ewe: Blessed one

Ogaasi   Ibo: If it goes well or ill people will say

Oganu   Ibo: We hear when it happens

Ogbo   WA: Companion

Ogbochukwu   Ibo: God's friend

Ogbonna   Ibo: The father's namesake

Ogbonne   Ibo: The mother's namesake

Ogechukwu   Ibo: God's time

Ogenno   Ibo: Mother's favor

Oginga   EA: One who drums

Ogobuihe   Ibo: To have an inlaw is to have a valuable possession

Ogochukwu   Ibo: Favour of God

Ogodimma   Ibo: It is good to have an In-law

Ogojinma   Ibo: It is the son-in-law who takes good care of his in-laws

Ogonna   Ibo: A favor from father

Ogubunka   Ibo: Warfare is an art

Oguerimba   Ibo: War does not wipe out a people
Ogujiofo   Ibo: Righteous fight
Ogunade   Yoruba: Ogun
Ogundana   Yoruba: Ogun blocks the way
Ogundeji   Yoruba: Ogun becomes two
Ogundiran   Yoruba: Ogun becomes hereditary
Ogungbade   Yoruba: Ogun receives a crown
Ogungbuyi   Yoruba: Ogun receives respect
Ogunlade   Yoruba: Crown
Ogunleye   Yoruba: Ogun has dignity
Ogunshoye   WA: Ogun has done well
Ogunsina   Yoruba: Ogun opens the way
Ogunsola   Yoruba: Ogun does an honorable thing
Oguntoyinbo   Yoruba: Ogun is stronger than white men
Ogwanbi   WA: Fortunate
Ohabuike   Ibo: Power resides in the people
Ohabuiro   Ibo: The people constitute one's enemy
Ohadiegwu   Ibo: People are wonderful
Ohadoo   Ibo: I plead with the people
Ohaegbum   Ibo: The people will not kill me
Ohaejighiuba   Ibo: People cannot prevent wealth
Ohaejiuba   Ibo: People cannot prevent wealth
Ohaejiugwo   Ibo: The people will not incur debt
Ohaerinwa   Ibo: Everybody cannot profit from a child
Ohajiuba   Ibo: But for the people wealth
Ohajiuka   Ibo: The people have to decide
Ohajunwa   Ibo: The people will not kill me
Ohakamadu   Ibo: The society is more important than the individual
Ohakwem   Ibo: May the people let me alone
Ohanyeaka   Ibo: May the people co-operate
Ohanyeaku   Ibo: May neighbors render help
Ohazom   Ibo: Let the people protect
Ohuuche   Ibo: Twenty thoughts
Ojealo   Ibo: He who goes and must return
Ojelabi   Yoruba: He is an Oje
Ojemba   WA: Traveller
Oji   Ibo: Giftbearer
Ojibuaku   Ibo: The Iroko tree is valuable cash crop
Ojiugo   Ibo: White kola
Ojo   WA: A child delivered with difficulty

Okang   EA: The first son
Okebugwu   Ibo: One obtains his share of anything for the sake of respect
Okechukwu   Ibo: The lot from God
Okediji   Yoruba: Hill becomes a refuge
Okeiyi   Ibo: A powerful stream
Okenwa   Ibo: Great child
Okeowo   Yoruba: Bag of money
Okera   WA: A likeness to God
Oko   WA: Elder of twins
Okolo   Ibo: Friendly
Okon   WA: Born in the night
Okoroafo   Ibo: Boy born on afo market day
Okorocha   Ibo: Okocha Fair complexioned young man
Okorukwu   Ibo: A big young man
Okpara   WA: Shelter
Okparanta   Ibo: A little son
Okparaoma   Ibo: Good son
Okparaukwu   Ibo: Big son
Okpueze   Ibo: Crown of a king
Okulaja   Yoruba: The Dead will settle the quarrel
Okunade   Yoruba: Cord of a crown
Okunola   Yoruba: Beads of honor
Okusanya   Yoruba: Power of the dead to avenge
Okwuanyimba   Ibo: Everything is negotiable
Okwuanyionu   Ibo: Nothing is too big for the mouth to utter/discuss
Okwubunka   Ibo: Speech is an art
Okwuchukwu   Ibo: The word of God
Okwudinma   Ibo: It is good to hold a talk
Okwudiuto   Ibo: Speech is pleasant art
Okwuoma   Ibo: Fair speech
Olabisi   Benin: Joy is multiplied
Olabisi   Yoruba: Joy
Olabummi   Benin: Honor has rewarded me
Olabuni   Yoruba: We are rewarded with honor
Oladapo   Yoruba: Honors are mixed together
Oladejo   Yoruba: Honors become eight
Oladiipo   Yoruba: Honors become many
Oladimeji   Yoruba: Honors become two
Oladunjoye   Yoruba: Honor is sweeter than titles
Oladunni   Yoruba: High status is sweet to have

Olaifa   Yoruba: High estate of an oracle
Olaiya   Yoruba: Mother's influence
Olalekan   Yoruba: It is expensive
Olaleye   Yoruba: Status have dignity
Olamina   WA: This is my wealth
Olanbiwonnnu   Yoruba: Our fame is causing them heartache
Olaniyi   WA: There's glory in wealth
Olaniyi   Yoruba: Glory
Olanrewaju   Yoruba: There is honor is moving forward
Olaolu   Yoruba: High estate of God
Olaoye   Yoruba: Highest honor
Olaseni   Yoruba: Fame and honor can be possessed
Olatunde   WA: Honor comes again
Olayinka   Yoruba: Honor surrounds me
Olebunne   Ibo: Which among them is the mother
Olejindu   Ibo: How many holds life
Olekaibe   Ibo: Who is greater than his fellows?
Olekanjo   Ibo: Which is worse than others
Olekanma   Ibo: Which is to be preferred
Olisakweadi   Ibo: There will be life if God permits
Oliver   French: From the olive tree grove
Oliver   Scandinavian: Kind, affectionate
Olivier   : The French form of Oliver
Ollie   : This diminutive for Oliver
Olodumare   Yoruba: Lord of splendour
Ololade   Yoruba: Here comes the honorable one
Olonade   Yoruba: Here comes the master artist
Olorode   Yoruba: Here comes the terrible one
Olorun   Yoruba: Lord of heaven: God
Olowo   Yoruba: Lord of Owo
Olowu   Yoruba: Lord of Owu
Olu   WA: Preeminent
Olubayo   : Greatest Joy
Olubunmi   Yoruba: God gave me
Oluchi   Ibo: The work of God
Oluchukwu   Ibo: The work of God
Olufadeke   Yoruba: God use a crown to pet this child
Olufemi   Yoruba: God loves me
Olufunke   Yoruba: A gift from God
Olufunlayo   Yoruba: God gave me joy

Olufunmilayo   Yoruba: God gives joy
Olugunna   Yoruba: God straightens the path
Oluigbo   Ibo: The word of the people
Olujimi   WA: God gave him to me completely
Olukoya   Yoruba: Champions of the cause of the suffering
Olulaanu   Yoruba: God have mercy
Olunfunke   Yoruba: God gives me to care for
Oluremi   Yoruba: God consoles me
Oluremi   Yoruba: God consoles me
Olusaanu   Yoruba: God the mercy
Olusanya   Yoruba: God compensates the suffering
Olusegun   Yoruba: The Lord breaks the resistance
Oluseye   Yoruba: God made an adornment
Oluseyi   Yoruba: God did this
Olusola   Yoruba: God deserves praise
Olutosin   Yoruba: God deserves to be worshiped
Olutoyin   Yoruba: God is deserves praises
Oluwole   Yoruba: Lord enters the house
Omagbemi   Shekiri: This child saved me Also Ogbemi
Omaone   Shekiri: I have a child
Omar   NA: Trustful
Omari   NA: Long life
Omavi   WA: The highest
Omenuko   WA: Acts at the time of scarcity
Omesede   Yoruba: A child is more than a king
Omodumbi   Yoruba: Children are sweet to have
Omolabake   Yoruba: It's a child we have beloved
Omolara   Yoruba: Born at the right time
Omolara   Benin: Born during the night
Omoleye   Yoruba: Children bring prestige
Omololu   Yoruba: Children are the summit of achievement
Omoniyi   Yoruba: Children bring prestige
Omorede   WA: Prince
Omorenomwara   Benin: This child will not suffer
Omorose   Yoruba: Beautiful child
Omorose   Benin: My beautiful child
Omoruyi   WA: Respect from God
Omosede   Benin: A child counts more than a king
Omosupe   Yoruba: A child is supreme
Omosupe   Benin: A child is the most precious thing

Omotunde   WA: A child comes again
Omowon   Yoruba: Children are dear
Omoyele   Yoruba: Children confer glory on a home
Omwokha   WA: The second of twins
Onajin   Yoruba: Soothing
Onefade   Yoruba: Here come the divinder
Oni   Benin: Desired
Onibiyo   Yoruba: On who has given birth rejoices
Onipede   Yoruba: Here comes the consoler
Oniyide   Yoruba: Here comes the dignified one
Ononikpe   Ibo: Is it under dispute?
Ononiwu   Ibo: Is it illegal?
Onuagbunwa   Ibo: Bad words do not kill a child
Onuamanwa   Ibo: A careless mouth that does not spare the child
Onubueze   Ibo: One can raise one's status by the way he uses words
Onubuogo   Ibo: Bad words can lead to a fight
Onuchukwu   Ibo: The word of God
Onuchukwu   WA: God's voice
Onukwuomma   Ibo: May people speak the right thing
Onumaegbum   Ibo: Bitter anger will not kill me
Onuwuegbum   Ibo: I shall not die yet
Onwuamaegbu   Ibo: Death kills the wrong persons
Onwuamaeze   Ibo: A careless tongue does not repsect the king
Onwuasanya   Ibo: Death is not a respector of persons
Onwuatuegwu   Ibo: Death is not a respector of persons
Onwubiko   Ibo: I plead with death
Onwubuariri   Ibo: Death is painful to one
Onwubuya   Ibo: Death is inexplicable
Onwudiegwu   Ibo: Death is a terrible thing
Onwudike   Ibo: Death is a strong blow
Onwuike   Ibo: Violent death
Onwujiuba   Ibo: Death disrupts prosperity
Onwukaike   Ibo: Death is more powerful
Onwuknjo   Ibo: If there is life there is hope
Onwumaihe   Ibo: Death does not kill at random
Onwunna   Ibo: Father's death
Onwunwa   Ibo: The worth of a child
Onyeasoibe   Ibo: Don't fear your fellow man
Onyebuagu   Ibo: Who is as strong as a Leopard?
Onyebuchi   Ibo: No man could be God

Onyebueke   Ibo: Who is the Creator?

Onyebuenyi   Ibo: Who is a friend

Onyedike   Ibo: Who is strong and powerful

Onyedimma   Ibo: Who is good

Onyedinma   Ibo: Who is good?

Onyedire   Ibo: Who is effective

Onyeike   Ibo: A strong man

Onyejiaka   Ibo: Who is sure

Onyejieke   Ibo: No one controls the creator

Onyejiuwa   Ibo: The world is not under human control

Onyeka   Ibo: Who is the greatest

Onyekachi   Ibo: No one is greater than God

Onyekachukwu   Ibo: Who is greater than God?

Onyekadibia   Ibo: Nobody knows more than the physician

Onyema   Yoruba: Sorrow

Onyemachi   Ibo: Who has seen God?

Onyemaechi   Ibo: Who knows tomorrow?

Onyemaenu   Ibo: Who knows what the heavens will bring

Onyemaizu   Ibo: No one understands the thoughts if others

Onyemauche   Ibo: Nobody understands the thought of others

Onyemeke   Ibo: Who understands the Creator?

Onyemenjo   Ibo: Nobody should do evil

Onyemobi   Ibo: Who knows the thought (of others)

Onyemoge   Ibo: Who knows the time?

Onyemuwa   Ibo: Who knows the way of the world?

Onyenso   Ibo: A holy man

Onyenweaku   Ibo: To whom belongs all wealth?

Onyenwuwa   Ibo: The world belongs to no one

Onyenyionwu   Ibo: Who is above death?

Onyesom   Ibo: Who is with me?

Onyewuchi   WA: Who is God

Opeolu   Yoruba: Gratitude to the Almighty

Oprah   AA: Famous black talk show host

Oraefo   Yoruba: Affectionate

Ordabro   Yoruba: Smooth sailingway

Ore   Yoruba: Gift of godess

Oredola   Yoruba: Friendship becomes an honor

Orenthal   English: Ornament "OJ" Simpson – Famous Athlete

Orion   Greek: Son of fire and light

Oriridinma   Ibo: Feasting is good

Orisajike   Ibo: All power belongs to God
Oriyomi   Yoruba: Saved by wits
Oronde   CA: Appointed
Orson   English: Son of the spearman
Orson   French: Little bear
Orville   French: From the golden estate or town
Osagboro   WA: Ther is only one god
Osage   WA: Whom God likes; loved by God
Osagie   WA: God agrees
Osahar   WA: God hears
Osakwe   WA: If God agrees
Osayaba   WA: God forgives
Osayande   WA: God owns the world
Osayinwese   WA: God created me all right
Osborn   German: Divinely strong Also Osborne
Oscar   Scottish: Warrior
Osei   WA: Maker of the great; noble
Oseye   Yoruba: The happy one
Oseye   Benin: A happy human being
Osifowora   Yoruba: Osi bought with money
Osinulu   Yoruba: Chief has a city
Osisiogu   Ibo: A tree that brings war
Osisioma   Ibo: Good tree
Osman   English: Protected of God
Osmond   Scandinavian: God's friend Also Osmin, Osmund, Oswin
Osondu   Ibo: Flight of life
Osonduagwuike   WA: Endless struggle for survival
Ossie   : A diminutive for names beginning with Os
Osuagwu   Ibo: Sacred to the agwu diety
Osuala   Ibo: The dedicated slave of earth goddess
Osuchukwu   Ibo: Devotee of God
Osuji   Ibo: Sacred to the yam God
Osuntoki   Yoruba: Osun River is enough to salute
Osuntokun   Yoruba: Osun is as big as the sea
Osuoha   Ibo: One sacred to the people
Oswald   German: Of divine power
Otegbeye   Yoruba: Civil strife attains diginty
Othiamba   WA: Born in the afternoon
Othieno   WA: Born in the night
Otolorin   Yoruba: He walked a different path

Otuome   WA: He does as he boasts
Overton   English: From the upper town
Owen   Welsh: Wellborn
Owodumni   Yoruba: Money is sweet to have
Owodunni   WA: It is nice ti have money
Owolabi   Yoruba: What money can do
Owoseni   Yoruba: Money is possible to own
Owusu   WA: The clearer of the way
Oyenuga   Yoruba: Titles have palaces
Oyesina   Yoruba: A title opens the way
Oyichukwu   Ibo: Friend of God
Oyinlola   Yoruba: Fame
Oyinola   Yoruba: Honorable estate
Ozibodi   Yoruba: Patience
Ozichi   Ibo: The message from God
Ozigbo   Ibo: The message for the people
Ozigbodi   Ghana: Patience
Oziogu   Ibo: Message of war
Ozioma   Ibo: Good news
Ozoekwen   Ibo: Another will not allow me
Ozoemem   Ibo: Another evil will not happen to me
Ozoememe   Ibo: Another evil will not happen
Ozooha   Ibo: Defender of the people
Ozumba   Ibo: A nations wealth
Ozzie   : A diminutive for Oswald
Paka   Swahili: Cat
Paki   Swahili: Witness
Palmer   Latin: Palm bearer, one who makes a pilgrimage carrying a palm
Pandu   NA: Artistic
Panya   Swahili: Tiny like a mouse
Panya   Yoruba: A twin child
Panyin   Fante: The first of twins
Parson   English: A minister who heads a parish
Paschal   French: Born at Passover or Easter; Pascal
Patire   WA: Where we are
Patrick   Latin: Noble one
Paul   Latin: Little
Payne   Latin: One from the country; Paine
Penda   Swahili: Admire
Pendo   Swahili: Love

Pepukayi   SA: We are alert
Perry   English: Wanderer
Pete   : A diminutive for Peter
Peter   Greek: Rock, stone
Petros   Greek: (Πετρος) Rock
Phil   : A nickname for Phillip rarely used as a given name
Philander   Greek: (Φιλανδρος) Fond of men
Philemon   Greek: (Φιλος) Friendship, Affectionate
Phillip   Greek: (Φιλιππος) A lover of horses
Pili   EA: The second child
Pili   NA: Second
Pili   Swahili: The second born
Polidore   Greek: (Πολιδωρος) Multiple gifts
Pongwa   NA: Cured
Popo   NA: Bat, sleeps in the daytime
Popoola   Yoruba: Highway to honor
Powell   Welsh: Son of Howell Often used as a surname
Prescott   English: One from the priest's dwelling
Pumla   SA: Now we can rest

Q

Qaadir   NA: Capable
Qaasin   NA: Just
Qays   NA: Logical
Quentin   Latin: Fifth child Also Quintin, Quinton
Quillan   Irish: Little cub Also Quillon
Quinby   Scandinavian: Dweller at the woman's estate
Quincy   French: From the fifth son's estate

R

Raaiwe   Ibo: Give up anger
Raanjo   Ibo: Abstain from sin
Raaobo   Ibo: Do not revenge
Raaokwu   Ibo: Avoid quarelling

Raashid   NA: Pious

Raawiya   Swahili: Story teller

Rabia   Swahili: Spring

Rabuwa   Swahili: Grow

Radford   English: From the red ford

Radhiya   Swahili: Agreeable

Rafael (rah fah EL)   Biblical: God has healed Also Raphael

Rafiya   Swahili: Dignified

Raha   NA: Comfort

Rahiim   NA: Merciful

Rahima   Swahili: Dompassionate

Rahma   Swahili: Compassion

Raisa   Swahili: President

Rajabu   NA: Born in the eight month

Rajalla   NA: God's wish

Ralph   English: Wolf counsel

Ramadhani   NA: Born in the Muslim month of fasting

Rami   NA: He is wise

Ramia   WA: Prophet

Ramla   Swahili: Divination

Ramla   Swahili: Predicts the future

Ramon   Spanish: Mighty protector; a form of Raymond

Ramsey   English: Dweller on the ram's island

Ramson   Latin: To redeem Fella Rasom Kuti – Famous Musician

Randall   : A form of Randolph

Randolph   English: Wolf shield

Raohiya   WA: Agreeble

Raoogu   Ibo: Avoid fighting

Raoul   : A French form of Ralph

Rapuluchukwu   WA: Leave it in God's hands

Rapuokwu   WA: Abstain from quarrel

Rashaad   NA: Righteous; Rashad

Rashida   Swahili: Intelligent; Righteous

Rasida   WA: Rightous

Rasidi   Swahili: Good council

Rasul   NA: Messenger

Rauf   NA: Merciful, Kind

Ray   French: An honored title

Rayan   Swahili: Rush

Rayburn   English: From the roe deer brook

Rayha   Swahili: Small comfort
Raymond   German: Mighty or wise protector
Razina   Swahili: Strong
Raziya   Swahili: Easy to get along with
Reem   Swahili: White antelope
Reeve   English: Steward
Reggie : A nickname
Reginald   German: Judicious, wise counselor, mighty and powerful ruler
Rehani   NA: Smell, basil, comfort
Rehema   Swahili: Of great compassion
Rehema   WA: Comparison
Rene   French: To rise again, to be reborn
Reuben   Biblical: Behold, a son Also Ruben
Rex   Latin: King
Rexford   English: The king's ford
Reynolds : A form of Reginald
Rhamah   EA: My sweetness
Richard   German Swahili: English Swahili: French: Powerful king; Richie
Richman   English: A powerful man
Richmond   German: Powerful protector
Ricky : A nickname for Richard that is occasionally used as a given name
Ridha   NA: Contended
Ridhwani   NA: Consent
Rifai   NA: Elevated
Rijaal   NA: Place of worship
Rikondja   SA: Our nation is struggling
Riley   Irish: Courageous
Riochi   Ibo: Ask from God
Rioelu   Ibo: Don't be ashamed to ask for favors
Rionna   Ibo: Ask your father for favors
Rionne   Ibo: Ask your mother for favors
Rioolisa   Ibo: Beg from the creator
Ripuree   SA: Think about this
Riziki   Swahili: Fortune
Robert   English: Bright with fame; Roby
Robin : This form of Robert is now more often used for girls
Rock   English: Dweller from the rock Also Roc
Rodman   German: Famous man English: One who clears the land
Rodney   Swahili: English: From the famous one's island
Roger   German: Famous spearman

Roland   German: From the famous estate; Rollie; Roland; Rollin
Romeo   Italian: Pilgrim to Rome;
Ron : A diminutive for Ronald
Ronald   German: Mighty, powerful
Roosevelt   Dutch: From the field of roses
Ross   Scottish; Dweller on the peninsula
Roy   French: King Irish: Red
Royal   Latin: King
Royd   Scandinavian: Dweller at the clearing in the forest
Rozi   Swahili: Flower
Rubama   NA: Possibility
Rubanza   NA: Courageous
Ruddie   German: Red
Rudo   SA: Love
Rudolph   German: Famous wolf
Rudy : A nickname for Rudolph
Rufano   WA: Happiness
Rufaro   SA: Happiness
Rufaro   Shona: Happiness
Ruford   English: Dweller at the red ford
Rufus   Latin: Red-haired
Rukiya   Swahili: She rises on high
Rukiya   Swahili: Superior
Rumaliza   NA: Deliverance
Runako   SA: Beauty
Russell   French: Red-skinned
Rutley   English: From the red meadow
Ruzuna   Swahili: Composed
Ryan   Irish: Kingly
Rylan   English: Dweller at the rye farm Also Ryland
Ryle   English: From the rye hill

S

Sa'ad   NA: Good fortune
Saada   Swahili: Happiness
Saada   WA: Help
Saadiya   Swahili: Happy
Saalim   NA: Safe

Saami   NA: Exalted
Saba : Shot form of Sabbatt
Sabiha   Swahili: Beautiful
Sabir   NA: Patient
Sabola   Brasil: Pepper
Sabra   Swahili: Patience
Saburi   NA: Patience
Sada Swahili: Help has come
Sade   Yoruba: Direct from God; Derived from the Yoruba name Olasade
Sadiki   NA: Trustworthy
Saed   NA: Happiness is here
Safa   Arabic: Clarity
Safaa   Swahili: Legibility
Safari   NA: Journey
Safe el-din   NA: Sword of the religion
Safiya   Swahili: Clearminded, pure
Safiya   Swahili: Purity
Safiyyah   Arabic: Serene
Safwani   NA: Sincere
Sagirah   Arabic: Little one
Saida   Swahili: Happy
Saidi   NA: Happy
Sakidi   WA: Faithful
Sakile   SA: Peace and beauty
Sakina   Swahili: Peaceful
Sakina   Swahili: Tranquility
Sala   EA: Gentle
Salah   NA: Good is a reward
Salama   Swahili: Peaceful
Salamuu   Swahili: Safe
Saleh   NA: Good
Salha   Swahili: Good
Saliim   NA: Safe
Salima   Swahili: Safe
Salima   Kenya: Safe corner
Salma   Swahili: Safe
Salmini   NA: Saved
Salome   Swahili: Safe
Salwa   Swahili: Consolation
Sam : Diminutive for names such as Samuel, Samson

Samiha   Swahili: Generous
Samiih   NA: Magnanimous
Samiir   NA: Companion
Samira   Swahili: Reconciler
Sampson : A variation of Samson
Samson   Biblical: Sun
Samuel   Biblical: His name is of God
Sanaa   Swahili: Art
Sanborn   English: Dweller near the sandy brook
Sancho   Spanish: Saint
Sanders : Sandy
Sandor   Slavic: He who helps others
Sanga   CA: He came from the valley
Sangeya   Shona: Hate men
Santana   Spanish: Saint
Sanura   Swahili: Kitten
Sara (Sarah)   Biblical: Joyful
Sara   NA: Gives pleasure
Sarahani   NA: Free
Sauda   Swahili: Of a dark complexion
Saul   Biblical: Asked by God
Saumu   Swahili: Fasting
Sauti   Swahili: Voice
Sazidde   Uganda: Fourth day
Scott   English: Dwells in Scotland
Scotty : Nickname for Scott Also Scottie
Sean   Irish: God is good; a variation of John
Sebold   English: Bold victory
Sebtuu   Swahili: Born on Saturday
Seeley   English: Happy, blessed
Sefu   NA: Sword
Seifred   German: Peace Also Seigfred
Sekai   WA: Laugh
Sekani   WA: Laughter
Sekayi   SA: Happy with laughter
Sekelaga   Nyakyusa: Rejoice
Sekou   WA: Fighter
Sekpuluchi   WA: Praise God
Selah   NA: Goodness
Selby   English: From the manor house

Seldon   English: Dweller in the willow tree valley
Selma   Arabic: Secure
Selwyn   English: Good friend Selvyn Selvin
Semaj   : Invented by african Americans
Semeni   Swahili: Speak
Sennett   French: Elderly, wise one
Sentwaki   EA: There is courage in him
Sereno   Latin: Calm, peaceful one
Serge   Latin: The attendant
Serwa   Ghana: Royal woman
Seth   Biblical: The appointed; the third son of Adam and Eve
Sexton   English: Church official
Sextus   Latin: Sixth son
Seymour   German: Victorious at sea
Sha-keith   : African American invented
Shaaahid   NA: Witness
Shaabani   NA: Ninth month
Shaba   NA: Morning has come
Shadeed   NA: Martyr
Shaffi   NA: Healer
Shafiiqa   Swahili: Amiable
Shahaab   NA: Shooting star
Shahida   Swahili: Witness
Shahrazad   Swahili: Princess
Shakila   Swahili: well-rounded
Shakwe   NA: Shoot up, growth, sprout
Shamakani   NA: Leader of the place
Shamba   Swahili: Plantation
Shambe   NA: Leader
Shamfa   EA: Sunshine
Shami   NA: Like the sun
Shamim   Swahili: Sweet scent
Shane   : This variation of Sean means the Lord is gracious
Shangwe   Swahili: Celebration
Shani   Swahili: Circumstance
Shannon   Irish: Wise
Shaquille   : African-American inventedinvented
Sharifa   Swahili: Distinguished
Sharifa   Swahili: Honorable
Sharifa   Ethiopia: Noble

Shariif   NA: Noble

Shaw   English: From the shady grove

Shawana   Swahili: Grace

Shazidi   NA: Growth

Sheikh   NA: Elder

Shelby   English: From the estate by the ledge

Sheldon   English: From the protected valley with steep sides; Sheldin

Shelley   English: Dweller at the ledge-meadow

Shelton   English: From the settlement near the high plateau

Shemsa   Swahili: Sunlight

Shep   : A nickname for Shepherd

Shepherd   English: An occupational name for one who tends sheep

Sherard   English: Brave

Sheridan   Irish: Wild man

Sherley   English: A bright path

Sherman   English: One who shears the sheep

Shermarke   WA: Bringer of good fortune

Sherwin   English: Good friend

Sherwood   English: From the shining forest

Shiba   Mali: Satiated

Shida   Swahili: Difficulty

Shifaa   Swahili: Cure

Shilingi   NA: money

Shiloh   Hebrew: The one to whom it belongs

Shiminege   Tiv: Let us see the future in this purity

Shinda   NA: Overcome

Shinuni   NA: Attack

Shomari   NA: Long and thin

Shoorai   Shona: Broom

Shujaa   NA: Brave

Shukuru   Swahili: Grateful

Shumba   SA: Lion

Shuruku   Swahili: Dawn

Sibadili   Swahili: I will not change

Sibby   : This diminutive for Sibley

Sibley   Latin: Prophetic

Sibongile   SA: Thanks

Sibusiso   SA: Blessing

Sid   : A nickname for Sidney

Siddell   English: From the wide valley

Sidney   French: From St Denis Also Sydney

Sifie   WA: We are dying

Sigele   Ogoni: Left

Sigidi   SA: He is like a thousand times

Sigolwide   Nyakyusa: My ways are straight

Sihaba   Swahili: Not a little

Siham   Swahili: I have not seen

Sihle   SA: Beautiful

Sikhumbuzo   SA: Reminder

Sikitu   Swahili: nothing

Sikose   SA: Tradition

Sikudhani   Swahili: I never thought

Sikujua   NA: I did'nt know

Sikukkun   WA: Born on Christmas

Sikumbuzo   SA: The ancestos remind us

Silas : A form of Sylvanus

Simana   NA: Stand up

Simangaliso   SA: He came quickly

Simba   NA: Lion

Simba   SA: Strength

Simeon   Biblical: Heard by God

Simiya   WA: Drought

Sims : Son of Simon

Simwenyi   WA: One who smiles every time

Sinaan   NA: Spearhead, brave

Sinclair   Latin: Illustrious French: From St Clair

Sipho   WA: A gift

Sipo   SA: A gift of love

Sisi   Fante: Born on a Sunday

Sitabua   NA: Her father loves her

Sithabile   SA: We are happy

Siti   Swahili: Lady

Siva   Hindi: Destroyer

Siwatu   Swahili: They are not our people

Siwazuri   Swahili: They are not good people

Siyasa   Swahili: Politics

Siyasa   Swahili: Politics

Siyazini   WA: What do we know?

Siyolo   SA: This is joy

Skeet   English: The swift one

Skerry   Scandinavian: From the rocky island
Skip   Scandinavian: Ship's owner Also Skippy, Skiper
Slade   English: Dweller in the valley Also Slayde
Smith   English: A worker with a hammer
Soaronna   Ibo: Follow your father's path
Soaronne   Ibo: Follow your mother's path
Socrates   Greek: The name of the great Greek philosopher
Soda   NA: Happiness
Sofolahan   Yoruba: The seer who exhibits fame
Sokoni   CA: He came from the sea
Solanke   Yoruba: A visionary
Solanke   Yoruba: It's a diviner we are looking after
Soleye   Yoruba: Dignity in vision
Solomon   Biblical: This son of David and Bathsheba
Solwazi   SA: He possesses wisdom
Somo   Swahili: Godmother
Somoe   Swahili: Her godmother
Somtochi   Ibo: Give praise to God
Sondai   SA: Keep pushing forward
Sondisa   SA: Bring him near to us
Songoro   NA: Smith
Sonnie   : Nickname meaning son
Soona   Ibo: Follow the father
Souchechukwu   Ibo: Follow the will of God
Souzochukwu   Ibo: Follow the way of God
Souzoma   Ibo: Follow the good way
Souzonna   Ibo: Follow the way of the father
Spencer   English: Provider
Spike   : A popular nickname Spike Lee, a filmmaker
Spiwe   SA: We were given
Ssanyu   Uganda: Happiness
Staajabu   Swahili: Surprised
Stacey   Latin: Stable, prosperous
Stafford   English: From the stony road
Stan   : A diminutive for Stanley
Stanley   English: From the stony meadow
Stara   Swahili: Protected
Stedman   English: Farmstead owner, dweller at the farmstead
Stephen   Greek: (Στεφανος) A crown
Steve   : A diminutive for Stephen

Steven   : An alternate spelling of Stephen
Stewart   English: An administrator
Stillman   English: Quiet
Stinson   English: Son of Stone
Stokely   : African-American invented
Stuart   : An alternate spelling for Stewart
Su'uud   NA: Good luck
Subria   Swahili: Patience rewarded
Sudi   NA: Good luck
Suhaila   Swahili: Ease
Suhailah   Arabic: Gentle
Sukutai   Shona: Squeeze
Sulaiman   NA: Solomon
Sulaymaan   NA: Peaceful Also Soloman
Sule   WA: Adventurous
Sullivan   Irish: Dark eyes
Sultaan   NA: Ruler
Sultan   NA: Authority
Sultana   Swahili: Ruler
Sulubu   NA: Tough
Sululu   NA: Consolation
Suluma   Swahili: Security
Sumai   NA: High
Sumait   NA: Reputable
Sumaiyya   Swahili: Good reputation
Sunna   Arabic origin
Sunny   Nickname of boys
Surayya   Swahili: Noble
Sutton   English: From the south estate
Suubi   Uganda: Hope
Suwedi   NA: Young master
Suwesi   NA: Govern
Sweeney   Irish: Little hero
Syandene   Nyakyusa: Punctual
Sylvanus   Latin: Forest dweller
Sylvester   Latin: From the wooded area

T

Taabu   Swahili: Difficulty
Taahir   NA: Clean
Taalib   NA: Seeker of knowledge
Taanisa   Swahili: Sociable
Tabansi   Jos: Endurance
Tabansi   Ibo: Endure patiently
Tabasamu   Swahili: Happiness
Tabia   Swahili: Habit
Tabia   Swahili: Talented
Tabita   Swahili: Graceful gazelle
Tabitha,Tabita   Swahili: Graceful
Tabor   Hungarian: From the fortified camp
Tacuma   CA: He is alert
Tad   Welsh: Father; an English nickname for Thaddeus
Tafida   Swahili: Graceful
Taghlib   NA: Overcome
Tagulani   SA: Be happy
Tahira   Swahili: Clean
Tahirah   Arabic: Pure
Tahiya   Swahili: Security
Tait   Scandinavian: Cheerful Also Taite
Taiwo   WA: First born of twins
Taiwo   Yoruba: First born of twins
Taiwo   Yoruba: Taste the world first
Takadiyi   SA: How are we doing
Taki   NA: God-fearing
Takiyah   Arabic: Righteous
Talbot   English: Bloodhound German: Valley bright Also Talbert, Tobert
Talha   Swahili: Easy life
Talup   EA: Friendship
Tamaa   Swahili: Greed
Tamiim   NA: Perfection
Tanabahi   Swahili: Be cautious
Tangeni   SA: Let us give praise
Tapfuma   SA: We are wealthy
Tarik   NA: Visitor
Tarrant   Welsh: Thunder
Taruvinga   SA: We have come for it

Tasie   WA: Be consoled
Tasieobi   Ibo: Be consoled
Tate   Native American: A great talker
Tathmina   Swahili: High value
Tatu   Swahili: Three times
Tausi   Swahili: Peacock
Tawfiki   NA: (Tawfiiq) divine guidance
Tawilu   Swahili: Tall
Taylor   English: An occupational name for a tailor
Taymur   NA: Manager, defender
Taymura   Swahili: Guardian
Tearle   English: Stern one
Tebogo   WA: Gratitude
Ted   : A diminutive for Theodore and Edward
Tefle   Swahili: Beginning
Teleza   Ogoni: Slippery
Temitayo   Yoruba: My life is a sufficient cause for joy
Temitope   Yoruba: My life is sufficient cause for gratitude
Terence   Latin: Smooth, polished one, tender
Terrell   English: Thunder Tirrell, Tyrell, Tyrelle,
Terris   English: Son of Terrill or Terence
Thaabit   NA: Firm, steadfast
Thair   NA: Honest and clean
Thako   WA: Hip
Thambo   WA: Ground
Thandiwe   SA: Beloved
Thani   NA: Second one
Tharwat   NA: Power
Thayru   Swahili: Thairu rebellious, furious
Thema   Akan: Queen
Themba   Zulu: One to be trusted
Thembeka   SA: Trustworthy is her name
Theo   : A diminutive for Theobald or Theodore
Theodore   Greek: (Θεοδωρος) Gift of God
Theophilus   Greek: (Θεοφιλος) Beloved by God
Thokozile   SA: Happiness
Thomas   Biblical: name used by many African parents
Tip   Biblical: A nickname for Thomas
Thuraia   NA: Star of my life
Thurgood   English: Good

Thurston   Scandinavian: Thor's stone Also Thurstan
Thuwayba   Swahili: Small gift
Thuweni   NA: Diminutive of second thani
Tichawoma   CA: We shall see
Timothy   Greek: He who honors God
Tindo   NA: Active
Titilayo   Yoruba: Happiness is eternal
Titilola   Yoruba: Endless honor
Tiwalade   Yoruba: Ours is the crown
Tobechuku   WA: Praise God
Tochukwu   Ibo: Give praise to God
Todd   Scottish: Clever, wily
Toju   Shekiri: God is all
Tolulope   Yoruba: To God belongs the glory
Tony   : Short for Anthony
Toola   WA: Workman
Toonna   Ibo: Give praise to father
Toonne   Ibo: Give praise to mother
Torbert   English: Form the bright hill
Torin   Irish: Chief
Torrance   Irish: From the knolls or little hills Also Torrence
Tosan   Shekiri: God knows the best
Townsend   English: Dweller at the town's end
Tracy   English: Courageous
Travis   English: Dweller at the crossroads
Trevor   Irish: Prudent, discreet, wise
Truman   English: A faithful or loyal man
Tsalani   WA: Good bye
Tshombe   AA: invented
Tsoyo   Shekiri: I'll take this joy
Tufaha   Swahili: Apple
Tuhfa   Swahili: gift
Tulimbwelu   Nyakyusa: We are in the light of God
Tulinagwe   Nyakyusa: God is with us
Tumaini   Swahili: Hope
Tumbo   NA: Stomach
Tumpe   Nyakyusa: Let us thank God for this child
Tumwebaze   Uganda: Let us thank God for this child
Tuni   Swahili: Tune
Tunis   Arabic: The capital of Tunisia

Tunu   Swahili: Novelty
Tupac   African-American invented
Turki   NA: Handsome, beloved, planet
Turkiya   Swahili: Beautiful
Turner   Latin: He works with a lathe
Tuwile   WA: Death is inevitable
Ty   : A short form for Tyler and Tyra
Tylan   African-American invented
Tyler   English: A house builder who makes tiles, bricks, and roofs
Tyoka   African-American invented
Tyra   Caribbean: Sweet person
Tyrone   Greek: (Θρονος) Sovereign
Tyson   English: Son of the Teuton

U

Uba   WA: Wealthy
Ubabuinye   Ibo: Wealth brings satisfaction
Ubabuoku   Ibo: Wealth comes through hardwork
Ubachuonwu   Ibo: Wealth does not prevent death
Ubadike   Ibo: It is hard to come into wealth
Ubadiuto   Ibo: It is pleasant to be wealthy
Ubanwa   WA: Wealth in children
Ubwa   NA: Delicate, young
Uchechi   Ibo: The will of God
Uchechukwu   WA: God's plan
Uchegbum   Ibo: Worries will not kill me
Ucheji   Ibo: Thoughts about yam
Uchendu   Ibo: Thought for life
Uchennabuisi   Ibo: The will of the father is paramount
Ucheoma   Ibo: Good will
Udeagha   Ibo: Rumors of war
Udeaku   Ibo: The importance of wealthy men
Udebuwa   Ibo: Fame makes life worthwhile
Udechukwu   WA: God's fame
Udegbulam   WA: May my fame not kill me
Udegbunam   Ibo: My fame may not constitute my destruction
Udego   Ibo: The importance of money
Udejiofo   Ibo: Campaign that relies on truthfulness

Udekogu   Ibo: Propoganda is more than the fight
Udekwem   Ibo: Fame is instructing me
Udell   English: From the yew tree valley Also Udel, Eudel
Udemgba   Ibo: The fame of wrestling
Udenwa   WA: Child's fame
Udo   WA: Peace
Udochi   Ibo: The peace of God
Udochukwu   Ibo: Peace of God
Udoka   Ibo: Peace is better
Udokanma   Ibo: Peace is better
Udueze   Ibo: The fame of the king
Udukwu   Ibo: A big drinking pot
Udunta   Ibo: A small drinking pot
Ufa   WA: Flower
Ugboaja   Ibo: Vessel for sacrifice
Ugboaku   Ibo: Vessel of wealth
Ugbogu   Ibo: Vessel of war
Ugo   Ibo: Eagle
Ugoagbulo   Ibo: Glory should not leave this house
Ugochi   Ibo: The glory from God
Ugochukwu : Eagle of God; illustrious
Ugodiegwu   Ibo: Itis great to be in glory
Ugodinma   Ibo: It is good to be glorious
Ugokwem   Ibo: May I be blessed
Ugwochi   Ibo: Reward from God
Ugwuadinjo   Ibo: Respect is a good thing
Ugwuchi   Ibo: Honor bestowed by God
Ugwumba   Ibo: The prestige of the people
Ugwunna   Ibo: The honor bestowed by father
Ugwunwa   Ibo: Dignity conferred by a child
Ugwuogu   Ibo: Fighting hill
Uju   WA: Abundance
Ukabiabia   Ibo: Trouble will never come
Ukadike   Ibo: The talk is difficult one
Ukaegbum   Ibo: I shall not be blamed to death
Ukaegbunwanne   Ibo: Quarrel should not end brotherhood
Ukaejem   Ibo: Gossips are not effective except at home
Ukagha   Ibo: A talk about war
Ukandu   Ibo: A talk about life
Uki   NA: Sadness, impediment

Ukwuoma   Ibo: Good luck
Uledi   NA: Young man
Uliss   : A variation of Ulysses also Ulice
Uliyemi   Shekiri: Home suits me Also Yemi
Ulooma   Ibo: Good home
Ulysses   Latin: Wrathful; Ulysses is the latin form of Odysseus
Umar   NA: Longevity Also Uma, Omar
Umayma   Swahili: Young mother
Umbaya   NA: Bad feeling
Umennabuike   Ibo: A living father is a source of strength
Umi   Swahili: my mother
Umi   WA: Life
Umkultum   Swahili: Prophet Muhammad's daughter
Umoja   NA: Unity
Umsa'ad   Swahili: happy mother
Umuabuka   Ibo: Children are not a source of quarrel
Umujigo   Ibo: Childrem constitute glory blessing
Unaegbunna   Ibo: Father is resistant to protestations
Unguja   Swahili: Zanzibar
Unis   : Derived from Eunice
Urbi   Benin: Princess
Uri   German: My light Also Urie
Uriel   German: Angel of light
Ursel   Latin: Strong as a bear
Urunna   Ibo: The benefits of having a father
Usaama   NA: Precious
Usi   NA: Hard
Uthman   NA: Third
Uvatera   SA: God help us
Uwadiegwu   Ibo: The world is wonderful/mysterious
Uwadiegwu   WA: The world is deep
Uwadinma   Ibo: The world is pleasant
Uwadiomimi   Ibo: The world is unfathomable
Uwaegbutta   Ibo: The world cannot overcome occasions for blame
Uwaekwem   Ibo: The people is fall of troubles
Uwaemenma   Ibo: The world are against me
Uwaezuoke   Ibo: The world is not perfect
Uwaezuoke   WA: The world is imperfect
Uwagboakwu   Ibo: People do not tolerate bad words
Uwakachi   Ibo: The world is no greater than God

Uwakweanu   Ibo: If the people of the world permits we will hear
Uwakwem   Ibo: May I thrive in the world
Uwanuokwa   Ibo: The world is heartless
Uwaoma   Ibo: Good world
Uwazeenjo   Ibo: May the world avoid sin
Uwdinjo   Ibo: The world is not a bad place
Uwimana   Rwanda: Daughter of God
Uwingabiye   EA: Sent by the diety
Uzoagbaoso   Ibo: The road is always there
Uzoaku   Ibo: The path of wealth
Uzoamaka   WA: Road is spendid
Uzoanuuli   Ibo: The path of happiness
Uzodinma   Ibo: The way/road is favorable
Uzoechiechi   Ibo: The way/line will not discontinue
Uzoechina   WA: May the road not close
Uzoezie   Ibo: The way has straightened
Uzoma   Ibo: Good way
Uzoma   WA: The right way
Uzondu   Ibo: The path that leads to life
Uzondu   WA: The way of life

V

Valantine   Latin: Strong
Vandell   African-American invented
Varick   German: Protecting ruler
Vernon   Latin: Born in the spring
Victor   Latin: Victorious, conqueror
Vincent   Latin: Conquering one Vinnie A nickname for Vincent
Virgil   Latin: Rod or staff bearer
Vuai   NA: Fisherman
Vuyelwa   SA: Joy
Vuyisa   SA: Made happy

W

Waafa   Swahili: accomplishment
Wadaran   African-American invented
Wade   English: From the river crossing
Wadell   African-American invented
Waduud   NA: Companion
Wagner   German: He builds wagons
Wahiba   Swahili: gift
Wahid   NA: Unique
Waiyaki   NA: Unto you
Wajihi   NA: Distinquished
Wakefield   English: From the wet field
Wakili   NA: Trustee
Walbert   English: Well-fortified
Waliid   NA: New-born child
Wallace   English: Man from Wales
Walt   : A diminutive for Walter
Walter   German: Powerful warrior
Walyam   Swahili: (William) protector
Wambui   EA: Singer of songs
Wamukola   WA: Left handed
Ward   German: Protector
Wardell   English: From the watchman's hill
Warren   German: Protector
Warrick   English: Stronghold
Waseme   Swahili: Let them talk
Watende   : No revenge
Watkins   English: Son of Walter Watson English: Son of Walter
Waverly   English: From the trembling aspen meadow
Wayne   English: Wagon builder
Waziri   NA: Minister
Wemusa   : Never satisfied with his wealth
Wesesa   Ewe: Careless
Weusi   NA: Black
Whoopy   African-American Invented
Willard   English: Bold, resolute
William   German: Resolute protector Willie A diminutive for William
Willis   English: Son of Will
Wilmer   German: Beloved, famous, and resolute

Wilmot   German: Of a resolute spirit
Wilson   English: The son of William
Wilver   African-American invented
Wimana   EA: He belongs to the diety
Winfield   English: From the friend's field
Winfred   African-American invented
Winslow   English: From the friendly hill
Winston   English: From the friendly estate
Winthrop   English: Dweller in the friendly village
Wolcott   English: From the brave man's cottage or wolf cottage
Wood   English: From the forest
Woodrow   English: Dweller at the hedge by the forest; Woody
Worley   English: Dweller at the uncultivated land
Worrell   English: Dweller at the true man's estate
Wright   English: A carpenter
Wudha   Uganda: Younger twin sister
Wuraola   Yoruba: Gold of Honor
Wylie   English: Charming

X

Xanthus   Greek: (Ξανθος) Golden-haired
Xavier   Spanish: Bright
Xhosa   SA: Give praises
Xylon   Greek: (Ξυλο) Dweller in the forest

Y

Yaa   Ghana: Born on Thursday
Yadikone   Wolof: You were here before
Yahimba   Tiv: There is no place like home
Yahya   NA: Lives, John
Yahya, John   NA: Living
Yakubu   NA: Jacob, James, Akub; blessed
Yaminah   Arabic: Proper
Yamro   CA: This one is courteous

Yao   SA: The unexpected truth
Yao   WA: Born on Thursday
Yardley   English: From the enclosed meadow
Yasmin   Swahili: Jasmine
Yassir   NA: Ease
Yathriba   Swahili: name for Madina
Yawa   WA: Born on Thursday
Ye   Ghana: Elder of twins
Yejide   Yoruba: She has her mother's face
Yero   CA: A Born soildier
Yerodin   CA: He is studious
Yetunde   Yoruba: Mother comes back
Yinka   WA: My own
Ynus   NA: Jonah
Yobachi : Pray to God
Yochanan   Hebrew: The Lord is gracious Yohanan A form of Yochanan
Yon   : Afican-American invented meaning Johanna
Yumna   Swahili: Good luck, happiness
Yusef   NA: The promise is true
Yusra   Swahili: Ease
Yusuf   NA: Joseph
Yuuthar   Swahili: Wealthy

Z

Zaafarani   Swahili: Saffron
Zacchaeus   Biblical: Clean Zach Diminutive for Zachariah Also Zack
Zachariah   Biblical: Jehovah has remembered
Zahor   NA: Blooming
Zahra   Swahili: Beautiful flower
Zahran   NA: Shine
Zahur   WA: Flower
Zahura   Swahili: Brightness, beauty, Venus
Zaid   NA: Abundance
Zaida   Swahili: Abundance
Zaina   Swahili: beautiful
Zainab   Swahili: Prophet Muhammad's daughter
Zainaby   NA: Prophet Muhammad's daughter

Zaituni   Swahili: olive, guava
Zakariya   NA: Rememberance; Zaccharias
Zaki   NA: Virtuous
Zakiya   Swahili: pure, righteous, excellent
Zakwani   NA: Thriving
Zale   Greek: Power of the sea
Zalika   NA: Born of good family
Zalika   Swahili: Well-born
Zalika   NA: New born
Zamani   Swahili: Long time ago
Zami   NA: The long journey
Zamoyoni   NA: From the heart
Zamzam   Swahili: holy spring
Zango   Central Africa: Good Dancer Zanza
Zarifa   Swahili: graceful
Zarina   Swahili: golden
Zawadi   Swahili: A gift has come
Zedekiah   Hebrew: The Lord is just
Zeenjo   Ibo: Avoid the evil
Zemmie   Greek: (Ζημωνω) Wine tapper
Zena   Swahili: beautiful ornament
Zenabu   Swahili: Beautiful
Zende   Congo: Strong and firm
Zeno   Greek: (Χενος) Hospitable Also Zenas, Zenon
Zenzele   SA: She will do it herself
Zera   Swahili: beauty, blooms, dawn
Zesireo   WA: Elder of twins
Zesiro   Cameroon: The firstborn twin
Zeyana   Swahili: ornament
Zihir   NA: Shining
Zihur   NA: Flowers are plentiful
Zina   Swahili: beauty
Zine   SA: I have four daughters
Zoe   Greek: (Ζωή) Life
Zoondu   Ibo: Save life
Zoonweigi   Ibo: Save yourself
Zubayda   Swahili: The best
Zubeda   Swahili: cream of the crop, wife, best
Zuber   NA: Brave
Zuberi   WA: Strong

Zuemma   Ibo: Think good thought
Zuga   SA: This too shall pass
Zugama   EA: Mother's favorite
Zugami   EA: Father's favorite
Zuher   NA: Shining
Zuhura   Swahili: Brightness
Zulekha   Swahili: Zulaykha brilliant, ahead
Zur   EA: The place to be
Zura   EA: Special touch
Zuri   NA: Good looking
Zurigama   EA: Mother's warm caress
Zuwena   Swahili: Small and beautiful

POPULAR MALE NAMES

A

Abam   Akan: Third born after the twins

Abanu   Ibo: I have joined the family

Abasi   Swahili: The stern one

Abayomi   Yoruba: Born to bring joy, or a ruler of people

Abbas   Arabic: A lion

Abdalla   Swahili: Servant of God

Abdu   Swahili: He worships God Also Abdul

Abdullah   Arabic: Servant

Abegunde   Yoruba: Born on a holiday

Abeid   Swahili: He is a leader

Abejide   Yoruba: Born in winter

Abena   Yoruba: He is pure

Abi   Yoruba: The royal guard

Abiade   Yoruba: Born to royal parents

Abidugun   Yoruba: Born before the war

Abiku   Yoruba: Changeling

Abimbola   Yoruba: Born of God

Abiodum   Yoruba: Born staunch opponent of during the festival

Abiodun   WA: Born at the time of a festival

Abiola   WA: Child born during first of the New Year

Abiola   Yoruba: Honorable

Abiona   Yoruba: Born on a Sunday

Abioye   WA: Born during coronation

Abioye   Yoruba: Born during the coronation

Abosi   WA: Life plant

Abosi   Yoruba: Life plant

Abu   Swahili: Nobility

Abu   WA: Nobility

Abubaka   Hausa: Noble

Abubakar   WA: Noble

Abwooli   Uganda: Catlike

Acholam   Ibo: Do not provoke me

Achufusi   WA: Do not reject

Acoli   Ibo: A son born after twins

Acque   Hausa: A tropical fruit

Adama   WA: Majestic

Addae   Akan: Beautiful as the morning sunrise

Addae   WA: Morning sun

Ade   WA: Crown

Ade   Yoruba: Royal

Adeagbo   Yoruba: He brings honor

Adebamgbe   Yoruba: Royalty has come to me

Adebayo   WA: He came in a joyful time

Adebayo   Yoruba: He came in a joyful time

Adeben   Akan: The 12th born

Adeboro   Yoruba: Royalty

Adedapo   Yoruba: Royalty

Adegoke   Yoruba: The year the crown has been exalted

Adejola   Yoruba: The journey

Adelaja   WA: A crown is added to my wealth

Adelaja   Yoruba: The crown settles a quarrel

Ademola   Yoruba: A crown is added to my wealth

Adetokumbo   Yoruba: Honor came from overseas

Adewole   Yoruba: Our crown has come home

Adeyemi   Yoruba: The crown suits him well

Adigun   Yoruba: He is righteous

Adika   Ghana: First child of a second husband

Adika   WA: First child of a second husband

Adio   Yoruba: He is righteous

Adisa   WA: One who makes himself clear

Adisa   Yoruba: He is precise

Adjua   Akan: He is noble

Adofo   Akan: The warrior

Adom   Akan: Help comes from God

Adunbi   Yoruba: Born to be pleasant, brings the people together

Adusa   Akan: The 13th son

Afi   Yoruba: Spiritual

Afibi   Yoruba: Born by the sea

Agibor   EA: Born in the wet season

Agyei   Akan: A messenger from God

Agyeman   Akan: The 14th son

Agymah   Fante: He will Become an expatriate

Ahmad   Arabic: One worthy of praise

Ahmed   Swahili: Praise worthy

Aiyetoro   Yoruba: Peace on earth

Ajagbe   Yoruba: He gets the prize

Ajamu   Yoruba: One who fights for what he wants

Ajani   Yoruba: One who takes possession after a struggle
Ajayi   Yoruba: Born facedown
Ajene   Yoruba: The truth
Akabueze   Yoruba: Support is paramount
Akamafula   Ibo: May my work be rewarded
Akanni   Yoruba: He brings possessions
Akiiki   Uganda: A friend, or born to be an ambassador
Akil   Arabic: Intelligent, one who reasons well
Akinkawon   Yoruba: Bravery pacified them
Akinlabi   Yoruba: We have a boy
Akinlama   Yoruba: He possesses valor
Akinlawon   Yoruba: Enduring bravery
Akins   Yoruba: He is a brave boy
Akinsanya   Yoruba: The hero avenges
Akinshegun   Yoruba: Valor conquers all
Akinsheye   Yoruba: Valor acts honorably
Akinshiju   Yoruba: Valor awakes
Akintunde   Yoruba: A boy has come again
Akinwole   Yoruba: Valor enters the house
Akinwunmi   Yoruba: Valor is pleasing
Akinyele   Yoruba: Valor benefits the home
Akna Fante: Born on Thursday
Ako   Yoruba: The first child is a son
Akobundu   Yoruba: Prudence is life
Akono   Yoruba: It is my turn
Akou   Yoruba: Wealth
Akram   Arabic: Most generous
Akua   Fante: Sweet messenger
Akuj   EA: High God
Akusa   Fante: Born on Thursday
Akwetee   Ga: Younger of twins
Alcoe   Hausa: A person of poor quality
Ali   Arabic: Exalted
Alimayu   Swahili: God is honored
Alonge   Yoruba: a tall and skinny boy
Amadi   Benin: Sick at birth to God
Ambakisye   Ndali: God has been merciful
Ambidwile   Nyakyusa: God has convinced me
Ambilikile   Nyakyusa: God called me
Ambonisye   Nyakyusa: God has rewarded me

Ameer Arabic: Commander, chieftan, or wealthy person
Ametefe Ghana: Born after his father's death
Amilcar Carthagenian One worthy of praise
Amin Arabic: Faithful
Amir Arabic: Populous
Amiri Swahili: Leader, ruler
Amobkile: Nyakyusa: God has redeemed me
Ampah Ghana: Trustworthy
Anane Akan: Our fourth son
Anapa Akan: Born in the morning
Andalwisye Nyakyusa: God has news for me
Andengwisye Nyakyusa: God has claimed me
Andongwisye Nyakyusa: God has led me
Angosisye Nyakyusa: God santified men
Anika Akan: Goodness has come
Animashaun Yoruba: He is generous
Ankoma Akan: Our last born
Anun Akan: Fifth born son
Anyabwile Nykakyusa: God has freed me
Anyelwiswe Nykakyusa: God has cleansed me
Aondochimba Tiv: God is above all things on earth
Apara Yoruba: A child comes and goes
Ara Hausa: The maker of Awotwe
Araam Hausa: Slender
Ashaki Yoruba: Beautiful
Ashon Ga: Seventh-born son
Ashur Swahili: Born during Islamic month of Ashur
Asim Arabic: Protector
Askia Mali: Askia Muhammad Toure, king of Songhay
Asma Arabic: Bold
Asukile Nyakyusa: The care of him
Aswad Arabic: Black
Ata Fante: Twin
Atat Somali: One who brings sunshine
Ategar EA: Tribes man
Atiba Akan: He is born with understanding
Atiim Akan: He is violent
Atsu Ghana: Younger of twins
Atta Akan: A twin

Atu   Fante: Born on Saturday
Ayinde   Yoruba: We gave praises and he came
Ayize   Zulu: Let it come
Ayo   Yoruba: Happiness
Ayodele   Yoruba: Joy has come
Ayubu   Swahili: Patience in suffering
Azagba   Benin: Born out of town
Azibo   Ogoni: Of the earth
Azikiwe   Ibo: Vigorous
Azizi   Swahili: Precious
Azubuike   Ibo: Support is strength

B

Baako   Yoruba: The first born
Babafemi   Yoruba: My father loves me
Babatu   Yoruba: He is a peacemaker
Babatunde   Yoruba: My father returns
Babatunji   Yoruba: My father returns again
Badru   Swahili: born at full moon
Badu   Akan: The tenth born child
Bahati   WA: Luck
Bakari   Swahili: Born with the promise of nobility
Bakesiima   Uganda: He has luck
Balewa   Ghana: He brings happiness
Balla   Arabic: Brave
Balogun   Yoruba: A warlord
Bamwoze   Uganda: The child is spoiled
Bandele   Yoruba: Born away from home
Banga   Shona: Sharp as a knife
Baraka   Swahili: Blessed
Baruti   Hausa: Be humble
Baruti   Tswana: Born to be a teacher
Baye   Yoruba: He is straightforward
Bayo   Yoruba: There is joy
Becktemba   Ndebele: He can be trusted
Bediako   Akan: He overcomes obstacles
Behanzin   Dahomey: He possesses strength and wisdom
Bejide   WA: Born during the rainy season
Bem   Tiv: He is peaceful
Bendo   Mende: He seeks fame

Beno   Nwera: One of a band
Betserai   Shona: Born to assist
Betta   Bobangi: He will sustain
Biboye   Ibo: You are what you want to be
Bisa   WA: He is greatly loved
Bloke   Yoruba: He is a proud chief
Bobo   Fante: Born on Tuesday
Bolewa   WA: He brings happiness
Bomani   Ngori: A warrior
Bongani   Ngori: He sings with joy
Boseda   Tiv: Born on Sunday
Brenya   Akan: I suffered before I got you
Bunwi   WA: Mygift
Buyinza   Uganda: God is mighty
Bwagilo   Nyakyusa: A source of things
Bwana   Swahili: Great master
Bwerani   Ogoni: Come child, you are welcomed
Byakatonda   Uganda: God owns everything
Byansi   Uganda: Baren earth
Byarugaba   Uganda: The giver's blessing

C
Camara   Greek: The square
Cara   Hausa: He in creases
Cata   Mende: A common plant
Cazembe   CA: He is a wise man
Cazembe   Central Region: A wise man is born
Chabwera   Ogoni: He has arrived
Chafulumisa   Ogoni: Hound
Changa   CA: Strond as iron
Changa   CA: Strong as iron
Changamire   CA: He is as the sun
Changamire   CA: Bright as the sun
Chatha   Ogoni: An ending
Chatuluka   Ogoni: A departure
Chekandina   Yao: Spicy
Chenzira   Shona: Born while his mother was traveling
Chiamaka   WA: God is splendid
Chibale   Ogoni: Kingship
Chibueze   Ibo: God is king

Chicha   Ibo: Beloved

Chidubem   Ibo: May God lead me

Chiemeka   Ibo: God has done much

Chigaur   Ogoni: The swift one

Chihambuane   Bachopi: Sweet potatoes

Chika   Ibo: God is the greatest

Chike   Ibo: Power of God

Chikosi   Ibo: God's work

Chikumbu   Yao: Knife handle

Chikwendu   Ibo: God gives life

Chilemba   Ibo: God will watch over His people

Chimanga   Ogoni: Maize

Chinelo   Ibo: Thought of God

Chinodu   Ibo: God is the protector

Chinua   Ibo: God's own blessing Chinua Achebe, famous author

Chinyelu   Ibo: Invincible

Chioke   Ibo: God, giver of talent

Chioma   Ibo: The good God

Chionesu   Shona: A guiding light

Chiosa   Ibo: God of all

Chiumbo   Mwera: A small creation

Chuckwuemeka   Ibo: Thank you, God

Chuma   Shona: He brings wealth

Chumachienda   Lomwe: A dignitary is on his way

Coblah   Ghana: Born on Tuesday

Coffie   Ghana: Born of Friday

Comas   Mende: He eats without sharing

Commenie   Hausa: He will exhort and persuade

Commie   Ghana: Born on Saturday Also Comie

Commo   Hausa: He has returned

Condy   Mende: A sugar plum Also Kondi

Congo   Mende: Reddish- brown Also Kongo

Coujoe   Ghana: Born on Monday

D

Dab   Mende: A small bird who weaves a nest in the grass

Dada   Yoruba: A boy child with curly hair

Dage   Hausa: Takes a firm stand Also Dago

Dakar   EA: One community

Dakarai   Shona: He brings happiness

Damani   WA: He is thoughtful

Danjuma   Hausa: Born on Friday

Danladi   Hausa: Born on Sunday

Darweshi   Swahili: He is like a saint

Daudi   Swahili: Beloved one

Dawud   Swahili: Beloved son

Dedan   Swahili: Town dweller

Deedum   Hausa: Pitchdark

Dehkontee   Bossa: Time will tell

Dia   Mende: He is a champion

Diaba   Mende: Cliff dweller

Diah   Hausa: Our offspring

Diah   Mende: A perching bird

Diallo   Mende: He is bold He is heroic

Diarra   Mende: A gift from God

Dibia   Mende: A healer is born

Diliza   Zulu: He destroys evil

Dingane   Zulu: He has needs The great

Diop   CA: Ruler, scholar

Diop   Wolof: Ruler Cheik Anta Diop – famous scholar

Djenaba   WA: Affectionate

Dunduza   CA: He will venture to see

E

Eba   Ngala: He under- stands

Ebere   WA: He will show mercy

Eberechukwu   Ibo: God's mercy

Ebi   Calabar: Good thought

Ebiowei   Calabar: A handsome boy

Ede   Ibo: Sweetness

Edo   Ibo: He is love

Ego   Ibo: Money

Ehioze   Benin: above all influence

Ejiikeme   Ibo: He will not use force

Ekeama   Ibo: Nature is splendid Also Ezikama

Ekechukwu   Ibo: God's creation

Ekundayo   Yoruba: Our sorrow becomes happiness

Ekwutosi   Ibo: Do not speak evil against others

Elel   Calabar: He comes like a cyclone

Elowea   Hausa: He comes like a cyclone

Enaharo   Benin: He shines like the sun
Enobakhare   Benin: The King's word
Entou   WA: He is a pearl
Epatimi   Calabar: A man of patience
Erasto   EA: A man of peace
Ewansiha   Benin: Secrets are not for sale
Eze   Benin: A king is born
Ezeamaka   Bini: A splendid king
Ezema   Ibo: The beloved chief
Ezenachi   Ibo: The king rules
Ezeoha   Ibo: The people's king

F
Fadil   Arabic: Generous
Fance   Hausa: To redeem
Fanta   WA: Born on a beautiful day
Fara   Hausa: Joy
Faraji   Swahili: He brings consolation
Farhan   Somali: One who brings happiness
Farih   Hausa: Bright light
Fati   Yoruba: He is robust
Fatou   Ga: He is beloved by all
Febechi   Ibo: Worship God alone
Femi   Yoruba: He will love me
Fenuku   Fante: A boy born after twins
Fenyang   Tswana: a conqueror
Fif;   Fante: Born on Friday
Foluke   Yoruba: This child is placed in God's hands
Fouad   Arabic: He come from the heart
Fudail   Arabic: A child of excellent character
Fulumirani   Ogoni: Born on a journey
Funsani   Ogoni: Request
Furaha   NA: happiness

G
Gahiji   Rwanda: The hunter
Gaika   Zulu: A gifted wood carver
Gamba   Shona: A warrior
Gambo   Hausa: A boy born after twins
Ganyana   Uganda: Born with the gift of patience

Garai   Shona: Be settled

Gata   Hausa: To be strong

Gerisa   EA: Strong as a leopard

Ghaniy   NA: Rich

Ginikanwa   Ibo: What is more precious than a child?

Goah   Swahili: Shield

Gogo   Nguni: He is like grandfather

Goredenna   Shona: Black cloud

Gowon   Tiv: Rainmaker

Gyasi   Akan: Wonderful

H

Habib   Arabic: The beloved

Habimana   Rwanda: God exists

Hafiz   NA: Guardian

Haji   Swahili: Born during the month of pilgrimage

Haki   NA: Justice

Haki   Arabic: Wise judge

Hakim   Arabic: He is wise

Hakim   NA: Judge Also Akeem

Hakizimana   Rwanda: It is God who saves

Hali   NA: Condition

Hamadi   Swahili: Praised

Hamid   Arabic: Thanking God

Hamisi   Swahili: Born on Thursday

Hamza   Arabic An important person out of history

Hanif   Arabic: True believer

Hannibal   Carthagenian: This ruler of Carthage

Haoniyao   Swahili: He doesn't see his own faults

Harambe   NA: Let's pull together

Harleem   Arabic: He is slow to anger

Harun   Arabic: Exalted

Hasan   NA: Good

Hasani   NA: Good

Hashim   Arabic: Crusher of evil

Hassiem   Arabic: He is strong

Hatari   NA: Danger

Helal   Arabic: Like the crescent

Hisham   NA: Generous

Hodari   NA: Expert

Hondo   Shona: He is prepared for war
Husani   Swahili: Handsome
Huseni   NA: Trustworthy

I

Ibrahim   Hausa: My father is exalted
Ica   Bini: The chief's necklace
Idi   Swahili: Born during Idi festival
Idogbe   Yoruba: Second born after twins
Idowu   Yoruba: Born after twins
Ifeancho   Yoruba: The desired child
Ifeanyichukwu   Ibo: Nothing is impossible with God
Ifoma   Ibo: A good acquaintace
Ihechukwu   Ibo: Light of God
Ikechuckwu   Ibo: The strength of God
Ikenna   WA: Father's power
Iman   Arabic: Preacher
Imarogbe   Benin: This child is born to a good family
Inaani   WA: Who is left at home?
Ipyana   Nyakyusa: Grace
Iroagbulam   Ibo: Let not enmity destroy me
Ishaq   Arabic: He laughed when he was born
Isma'iil   NA: He hears Also Ismail
Issa   Arabic: God is our salvation
Isukanma   Yoruba: May the future be bright
Iyapo   Yoruba: Child of many trials

J

Jabali   NA: Strong as a rock
Jabari   Swahili: He is brave
Jabir   NA: Restorer
Jabulani   Ndebele: Be happy
Jafari   Swahili: A creek
Jahi   Swahili: He has dignity
Jaja   Ibo: He is honored
Jalaal   Arabic: Majestic
Jaleel   Arabic: Illustrious
Jaleel   White is an actor
Jalil   NA: honorable
Jama   Somali: One who brings people together

Jamaal   Arabic: He is beauty
Jamal   NA: Elegance
Jameel   Arabic: Physically and morally attractive
Jamili   NA: Handsome
Janna   Hausa: A cord used for decoration
Jaramogi   EA: He travels often
Jauhar   NA: A Journey
Jawanza   CA: This one is dependable
Jawanza   C A: This one is dependable
Jawara   Hausa: Peace loving
Jawhar   Arabic: Ghanal
Jela   Swahili: His father was in prison at birth
Jibade   Yoruba: Born close to royalty
Jimiyu   Uganda: Born in a dry season
Jojo   Fante: Born on Monday
Juma   NA: Born on Friday
Juma   Swahili: Born on Friday
Jumaane   Swahili: Born on Tuesday
Jumoke   Yoruba: Everyone loves this child
Jurodoe   Bassa: Faithful
Jurude   Bassa: Justice; fairness
Kadugala   Uganda: He is very black
Kafele   Ogoni: He is worth dying for
Kafuko   Uganda: A child born after a deceased sibling
Kaga   Hausa: The pick of the bunch
Kahero   East Africa: Conceived at home
Kailugaru   Uganda: He is very dark
Kakuyon   CA: He arms the people
Kakuyon   CA: Maker of weapons
Kala   WA: Tall
Kalawa   Yao: Flowers
Kalif   Somalia: Holy Boy
Kalindaluzzi   Uganda: The well keeper
Kalonji   CA: He will be victorious
Kalonji   CA: Man of victory
Kamau   Ogoni: Quiet warrior
Kambui   EA: Fearless
Kambuji   Ogoni: Goat
Kamowa   Ogoni: Beer
Kanko   Hausa: You are able to do

Kanyama   CA: Guard
Kapeni   Ogoni: Sharp as a knife
Karanja   EA: Guide
Kariamu   EA: One who reflects the almighty
Karume   EA: Keeper of the forest
Kashka   Yoruba: He is friendly
Kasimu   WA: Keeper of the forest
Katambu   Uganda: The chief
Katayira   Uganda: Not staying in one place
Katorogo   Uganda: The premature child
Kawabena   Akan: Born on Tuesday
Kaya   Akan: This child is a laborer
Kayode   Yoruba: He brought joy
Kazandu   Zulu: You are a young man
Kazembe   Yao: He is an ambassador
Kazungu   Uganda: Light skinned child
Keambiroiro   Kikuyu: Mountain of blackness
Kefentse   Tswana: Conqueror
Kehinde   Yoruba: The second born of twins
Keita   Fulani: Worshipper
Kenyatta   Kikuyu: A musician
Kenyetta   EA: Sound of beautiful music
Kereenyage   Kikuyu: Mountain of mystery
Kesi   EA: Born at a time when father worked hard
Ketecumbeh   Mano: Grow up and provide
Ketema   EA: From the valley
Ketto   Hausa: Sunrise
Kgosie (HO sie)   Xhosa: Born in South Africa
Khaalid   Arabic: Durable,
Khaldun   Arabic: Eternal
Khalfani   Swahili: He is destined to rule
Khama   Botswana: The good king
Khamisi   Swahili: Born on Thursday
Khari   Swahili: Kingly
Khatiti   EA: Sweet little thing
Kiah   Bobangi: Always
Kiambu   Kikuyu: This boy will be rich
Kiamni   Swahili: Sailor
Kibumba   Uganda: Creator
Kifimbo   Swahili: A very thin baby

Kigongo   Cameroon: Born before twins
Kitaka   CA: Good farmer
Kitwana   Swahili: Pledged to live
Kiyumba   Uganda: Morning sun is sweet
Kizza   Cameroon: Born after twins
Kobie   WA: Warrior
Kodjo   WA: Humorous
Kodwo   Twi: Born on Monday
Kofi   Twi: Born on Friday
Kojo   Akan: Born on Monday
Kojo   Yoruba: Unconquerable
Kokayi   Shona: Summon the people to hear
Koma   Bobangi: Mature
Konata   Yoruba: A man of high station
Kondo   Swahili: War
Kondwnai   Ogoni: Joyful
Kontar   Akan: An only child
Kopano   Tswana: Union
Kpodo   Ghana: Elder of twins
Kufere   Yoruba: Do not forget
Kufuo   Fante: His father shared the birth pains
Kunle   Yoruba: His home is filled with honors
Kwacha   Ogoni: Morning
Kwada   Ogoni: Night has fallen
Kwadwo   Akan: Born on
Kwakou   Ghana: Born on Wednesday
Kwame   Akan: Born on Saturday
Kwayera   Ogoni: Dawn
Kweisi   Ga: A golden child
Kwende   Ogoni: Let's go
Kwesi   Akan: Born on Sunday

L
Lafte   Hausa: Thin
Lamburia   Ogoni: Clean bush
Lasana   CA: A poet of the people
Lasana   CA: A poet of the people
Lateef   Arabic: Gentle, pleasant on one
Layla   EA: Born at night
Laze   Arabic: Blaze

Leabua   Sotho: You speak
Linhanda   Uganda: A Broadway
Lishe   Hausa: Born at midnight
Lisimba   Yao: The lion
Lnaduleni   Ndebele: One who finds greatness
Lukman   Arabic: A prophet is among us
Lulu   EA: She is a pearl
Lumo   Ghana: Born facedown
Lumumba   Bokango: Gifted, brilliant- Patrice Lumumba
Lumumba   CA: Gifted, brilliant
Lutalo   Cameroon: A warrior
Luttakkome   Nugwere: Who talks much
Luzige   Mugwere: Locust
Lwandeka   Muwere: Locust

M
Maajid   Arabic: Honorable
Maalik   Arabic: Master Also Malik
Madzimoyo   Ogoni: Water of life
Magezi   Uganda: A boy who is wise
Magomu   Cameroon: Younger of twins
Majeed   Arabic: Noble
Makami   Hausa: He seizes
Maklani   Mweri: One skilled in writing
Mani   CA: He came from the mountain
Mansa   Mali: Mansa
Manu   Akan: Born second Manu Dibango, popular saxophonist
Mapira   Yao: Millet
Masamba   Yao: He leaves
Mashama   Shona: You are surprised
Masibuwa   Yao: Modern days
Maskini   Swahili: Poor
Masomakali   Nyakyusa: Sharp eyes
Masud   Swahili: Fortunate
Matsimela   Sotho: Roots
Maulidi   EA: Born during the month of Maulidi
Mawulawde   Ghana: God will provide
Mawuli   Ghana: There is a God
Mazi   Ibo: Sir Mazie as used by African-Americans

Mbita   Swahili: Born on a cold night

Mbiya   Yao: Money

Mbizi   Lomwe: To drop in water

Menelek   Ethiopia: Menelek II, king of Abyssinia from 1844 to 1913

Mensah   Ghana: Third son

Mhina   Swahili: Delightful

Micere   EA: Has a strong will

Mijiza   EA: Works with her hands

Minkah   Akan: Justice

Molefi   Swahili: The keeper of tradition

Mongo   Yoruba: Famous

Montsho   Tswana: Black

Mosegi   Tswana: Tailor

Mosi   Swahili: Firstborn

Mosi   EA: She is the first born

Moswen   Tswana: Light in color

Moyo   Ogoni: Life, wellbeing, good health

Mposi   Nyakyusa: Blacksmith

Mpyama   CA: He shall inherit

Mthuthuzeli   Xhosa: Comforter

Mtima   Ogoni: Heart

Mudada   Shona: The provider

Muga   EA: Mother of all

Mugabe   CA: Intelligent, quick

Mugabe   Shona: He is intelligent and quick

Muhammad   Arabic: Worthy of praise

Muka   Bobangi: We harvest

Mukawano   Uganda: A boy who is loved

Mukumtagara   EA: Born at war time

Mukumutara   EA: Born during Mutara

Musana   Uganda: Born during the daytime

Mutope   CA: Protector

Mwai   Ogoni: Good fortune

Mwamba   Nyakyusa: Strong

Mwanze   Swahili: The child is protected

Mwinyi   Swahili: King

Mwinyimkuu   Zaramo: Great king

Mwita   Swahili: He summons the people

N

Naama   Hausa: Sweet Herbs Also Namon
Nadifa   EA: Born between seasons
Naeem   Arabic: Benevolent
Nafula   EA: Born during raining season
Naisb   Somalia: The lucky one
Najjam   Uganda: Born after twins
Najuma   EA: She abounds in joy
Nakisisa   Muguda: Child of the shadows
Nando   Mende: A variety of okra
Nangila   Abaluhya: born while parents were travelling
Nangwaya   Mwera: Don't trifle with me
Nassor   Swahili: Victorious
Ndale   Ogoni: Trick
Ndembo   Yao: Elephant
Ndidi   Ibo: Patience
Ndulu   Ibo: Dove
Ndweleifwa   Nyakyusa: I came with the morning
Ngicuro   EA: Born in the plains
Ngimonia   EA: People of the forest
Ngoli   Ibo: Happiness
Ngozi   Ibo: Blessing
Ngunda   Yao: Dove
Niamke   Yoruba: God's gift
Nikusubila   Nyakyusa: Hopeful
Nilotes   EA: Born at the river Niger
Njeri   EA: Daughter of a warrior
Nkosi   Zulu: Ruler
Nkuku   Yao: Rooster
Nkundinshuti   Rwanda: One who likes his friends
Nogomo   CA: He will appear
Nsekanabo   Uganda: Boy who likes people
Ntoko   Bobangi: Professional ability, dexterity
Ntoma   Bobangi: Messenger
Nuru   Swahili: Born in daylight
Nyamekye   Akan: God's gift

O

Oba   Benin: Ruler Yoruba: King
Obadele   Yoruba: The king arrives

Obafemi   Yoruba: The king likes me
Obaskei   Benin: The king's influence is far reaching
Obataiye   Yoruba: King of the world
Obawole   Yoruba: The king enters the house
Obayana   Yoruba: The king warms himself
Oboi   Acoli: Second son
Odai   Acoli: Third son
Ode   Benin: Born along the road
Ogbonna   Ibo: Image of his father
Ogolu   Ibo: He came at the right time
Ogorchuckwu   Ibo: Gift of God
Ojore   Ateso: A man of war
Ojuneku   Ibo: The Lord has spoken
Okang   Acoli: First son
Okanlawon   Yoruba: Son born after several daughters
Okechuku   Ibo: God's gift
Oko   Ga: Elder of twins
Ola   Yoruba: Wealth, riches
Oladele   Yoruba: Wealth arrives
Olafemi   Yoruba: Wealth favors me
Olamina   Yoruba: This is my wealth
Olaniyan   Yoruba: Honor surrounds me
Olaniyi   Yoruba: There is glory in wealth
Olatunji   Yoruba: Honor reawakens
Olu   Yoruba: Preeminent
Olubayo   Yoruba: Highest joy
Oluchuckwu   Ibo: The handiwork of God
Olufemi   Yoruba: God loves me
Olujimi   Yoruba: God gave me this
Olushola   Yoruba: God has blessed
Olutosin   Yoruba: God deserves to be praised
Oluwa   Yoruba: Our Lord
Oluyemi   Yoruba: Fulfillment from God
Omar   Arabic: The highest
Omolara   Benin: Child born at the right time
Omorede   Benin: Prince
Onipede   Yoruba: The consoler is come
Onyoka   Ibo: Who is the greatest?
Oree   Benin: Corncake
Orji   Ibo: Mighty tree

Osagboro   Benin: There is only one God
Osahar   Benin: God hears
Osakwe   Benin: God agrees
Osayaba   Benin: God forgives
Osayande   Benin: Almighty
Osayimwese   Benin: God made me whole
Osaze   Benin: Whom God Likes
Osei   Fante: Noble Osei
Othiambo   Luo: Born in the afternoon
Othieno   Luo: Born at night
Ottah   Urhobo: Child born immatiated
Owodunni   Yoruba: It is nice to have money
Oza   Bini: Metal
Ozoma   Ibo: Another good turn

P
Paki   Xhosa: Witness
Pereya   Ibo: God's gift or blessing
Petiri   Shona: Where we are
Pili   Swahili: The second born child

Q
Quaashi   Ghana: Born on Sunday

R
Rachiim   Persian: Seed of rulership
Ramni   Arabic: He is wise
Rashidi   Swahili: Of good council
Rhamah   EA: My sweetness
Roble   Somali: Rain maker
Rudo   Shona: Love
Runako   Shona: Hand- some
Runihura   Rwanda: Victorious

S
Saabir   Arabic: One who patiently endures hardships
Saabola   Ogoni: Pepper
Saadiq   Arabic: Faithful, a man of his word Also Sadiq
Sabir   NA: Patient
Sadiki   Swahili: Faithful, sincere, a man of truth

Saidi   NA: Happy

Sala   EA: Gentle

Salehe   Swahili: Good, righteous

Salim   Swahili: Peaceful

Sango   Bobangi: Father

Seba   Ngali: To know, understand

Sebahive   Rwanda: Brings good fortune

Sefu   Swahili: Sharp as a sword

Sekani   Ogoni: Full of laughter

Sekou   Toure is the beloved leader of Guinea

Sekou   WA: Great warrior, fighter, leader

Sentwali   Rwanda: Brave

Shadeed   NA: Martyr

Shaka   Zulu: Shaka became king of all the Zulus in 1818

Shamba   Congo: Shamba

Shinda   NA: Overcome

Shomari   Swahili: Forceful personality

Shumba   Shona: Lion

Simana   NA: Stand up

Simba   Swahili: Lion

Sipho   Zulu: A gift

Sipliwo   Xhosa: A gift

Siyolo   Zulu: This is joy

Solwazi   Swahili: He is knowledge

Sondisa   Shona: Bring him near to us

Sonigah   Bassa: Boychild born on Sunday

Ssanyu   Uganda: He brings happiness

Sudi   Swahili: Good luck

Suhuba   Swahili: A good friend

Sulaymaan   NA: Peaceful Also Soloman

Sultan   NA: Authority

Sultan   Swahili: Ruler

Sundai   Shona: Keep pushing forward

Sundiata   Fulani:

Sundiata   EA: Keita was a 14th-century leader in the kingdom of Mali

Sunna   Arabic: Skillful man

Sunni   Sudan: Sunni Ali Ber, king of Songhay

Suubi   Uganda: He brings hope

T

Tacuma   CA: He is alert

Taiwo   Yoruba: The elder of twins

Talib   Arabic: A seeker

Talup   EA: Friendship

Tau   Tswana: Lion

Tenywa   Uganda: Younger twin brother

Thabiti   Mwera: A true man

Thankdiwe   Zulu: Beloved

Themba   Xhosa: Hope

Tichawona   Shona: We shall see

Toma   Mende: Significant

Tshepo   SA: The concerned

Tumaini   Mwera: Hope

Tumwebaze   Uganda: Let us thank God

Tumwijuke   Uganda: Let us remember God

Tuponile   Nyakyusa: We are saved

Tusabomu   Uganda: We give thanks to God

Twia   Fante: Born after twins

Tyehimba   Tiv: We stand as a nation

U

Uba   Ibo: Wealthy

Ubanwa   Ibo: Wealth in children

Uchachuckwu   Ibo: God's sense, or God's plan

Umi   Yao: Life

Umoja   NA: Unity

Unika   Lomwe: Light up

Useni   Yao: Tell me

Uuka   Xhosa: Wake up

Uwaboufu   Ibo: The world is one

V

Vuai   Swahili: Savior

W

Wabwire   Uganda: Born at night

Wafula   Uganda: Born during the rain

Wakili   NA: Trustee

Wambuzi   Uganda: Mr Goat

Wamukota   Abaluhya: Left-handed
Watende   Nyakyusa: There is no revenge
Weke   Ibo: Born on Eke market day
Wemusa   Cameroon: Never satisfied with his possessions
Weusi   NA: Black

Y

Yafeu   Fante: He is bold
Yahya   Swahili: God's gift
Yahya, John   NA: Living
Yao   Ghana: Born on Thursday
Yawo   Akan: Born on Thursday
Yohance   Hausa: God's gift
Yoofi   Akan: Born on Friday
Yooku   Fante: Born on Wednesday
Yorkoo   Fante: Born on Thursday
Yusef   Arabic: His power increases
Yusuf   NA: Joseph
Yusuf   Swahili: He shall add to his powers
Yusufu   Swahili: This one charms

Z

Zahur   Swahili: Flower
Zambga   Bossa: Firstborn
Zami   NA: The long journey
Zikusooka   Uganda: Better to suffer early in life than later
Zuberi   Swahili: Strong
Zuka   Shona: Sixpence

POPULAR FEMALE NAMES

A

A'Lelia : African-American

Aba   Fante: Born on Thursday

Abam   Akan: Next child

Abayaa   Akan: Born on Yawda (Thursday)

Abayomi   Yoruba: She brings joy

Abba   Swedish: Free like a bird

Abbey   French: A diminutive for Abigail Also Abbie, Abby, Abbe Abbey

Abebi   Yoruba: Delivered

Abeje   Yoruba: We asked to have her

Abeke   Yoruba: To be loved

Abena   Ashanti: Tuesday's

Abenaa   Akan: Born on Tuesday

Abeni   Yoruba: Behold she is ours

Abeo   Yoruba: Born with wealth

Abiah   Ibo: Visitor

Abiba   NA: The beloved one

Abidemi   Shekiri: Refined

Abigail   Biblical: My father rejoices

Abimbola   Yoruba: Born to be rich

Abina   Akan: Born on Thursday

Abiola   Yoruba: Born in honor

Abir   Arabic: Fragrant

Ablah   Arabic: Perfectly

Abriana   Italian: The feminine form of Abraham

Abwooli   Uganda: Cat

Ada   German: Happy, prosperous Also Aida

Adah   Ibo: First daughter

Adaline : A variation of Adeline

Adamina   French: The feminine form of Adam

Adanma   Yoruba: A beautiful daughter

Adanna   Yoruba: Father's daughter

Adanne   Yoruba: Mother's daughter

Adaoha   Yoruba: Daughter of the people

Ade   Yoruba: Short for names beginning with Ade. E.g. Adewomi

Adela : A little-used short form of Adelaide; Adell, Adelia

Adelaide   Swahili: Nobility

Adele   German: Noble Also Adelle, Adellah, Adell

Adeleke   Yoruba: The crown brings happiness

Adeline   : One of the numerous adaptations of Adelaide

Adelphi   Greek: (Αδελφι) Sisterhood

Adeola   Yoruba: Born with a crown

Aderinola   Yoruba: Crowned

Adero CA: She gives life

Adia   Swahili: A gift from God has come

Adiba   Arabic: She is born in want of parents

Adina   French: Adornment also Adeana, Adine

Adira   French: Noble, powerful

Adiva   Arabic: Gentle

Adoa   Akan: Born Saturday

Adona   : The feminine of Adonis

Adonica   Spanish: Sweet

Adorna   English: To adorn

Adrana   : This name appears to be of recent invention; Adrena, Adrenia

Adrienne   Latin: Dark one; the feminine form of Adrian

Aduke   Yoruba: Plentiful

Adun   Shekiri: I struggle

Adunni   Yoruba: Sweet

Adwoa   Akan: Born on Monday

Adwoa   Fante: Born Monday

Aesha   Swahili: Life, prosperous Also Aisha

Afafa   Ghana: First child of second husband

Afiya   Swahili: Healthy

Afra   Arabic: White

Afua   Ghana: Born on Friday

Agatha   Greek: (Αγαθη) Good

Agnes   Greek: (Αγνη) Pure, virginal

Ahlam   NA: Dreams

Aida   Arabic: Reward

Aileen   Irish: Light

Aimee   French: Beloved

Aina   Yoruba: Surrounded by mystery

Aisey   : African-American invented

Aisha   NA: Life

Aisha   Swahili: Life

Aishah   Arabic: Prosperous

Akanika   Yoruba: Born during the festival

Akata   Yoruba: Strong headed

Akatwijuka   Uganda: God alone

Akenke   Yoruba: Precious daughter

Akiki   Uganda: Ambassador

Akilah   Arabic: Bright

Akili   Ibo: Born strong

Akos   Akan: Born on Sunday

Akosua   Ghana: Born on Sunday

Alair   Greek: (Αλαια) Cheerful

Alake   Yoruba: She will be loved if she lives

Alana   French: A feminine form of Alan

Alandra   Spanish: A form of Alexandra

Alanza : A feminine form of Alonzo

Alberta   German: Noble shining: the feminine form of Albert

Albertina : Used a lot during the early 19th century

Alcenia   Greek: (Αρχινια) Good beginning

Aldara   Arabic: Winged gift

Aldina   German: Old Also Alda, Aldine, Aldyne, Aleda

Aldona   German: The old one

Aldonza   Spanish: Sweet

Aldora   English: Noble gift

Alero   Shekiri: The earth is fertile

Aleta   Greek: (Αληθεια) Truth Also Aletha

Alexa : A feminine form of Alexander

Alexis : Greek: Defender

Alfre : A diminutive for Alfreda

Alfreda : The feminine form of Alfred Also Alfreeda

Alice   German: Noble Also Alecia, Alicea, Alicia, Alisha

Alike   Yoruba: She is my favorite

Alile   Yao: She weeps

Alima   Arabic: Cultured

Alina   Slavic: A variation of Helen

Alison : Popular name Also Allison

Aliyah   Arabic: Exalted

Alma   Latin: Born generous

Almeda   Latin: one who is focused and achieves

Almeta : A variation of Almeda

Almira   Arabic: Princess, exalted

Alona   Spanish: Strong as an oak tree

Alphonsine : Feminine version of Alphonso

Alta   Latin: Elevated

Altamase : A variation of Alta Also Altha
Althea   Greek: (Αλθεα) Wholesome
Altonia : Popular with Southerners in the early 18th century
Altoria : African American Invented
Altovise   Greek: (Αλτοβια) Personable woman
Alva   Hebrew: Brightness
Alvena   Feminine version of Alvin
Alverda   Spanish originated
Alvira   Spanish originated
Alzarah   Native American: Tip of a mountain
Alzena   Arabic: Woman
Alzera   Native American originated
Alzetta   Mexico: Thrudding of a horse
Alzora : Originated from Mexico
Ama Akan   Swahili: Ghana: Born on Saturday
Amadi Ibo: Giant
Amadoma   Akan: Born on Saturday
Amal   NA: Hopes
Amanda   Latin: Worthy of much love
Amani   Arabic: Aspiration
Amaretta : Latin Origin
Amber   French: A semiprecious gem
Amelia   German: Industrious
Amia   Italian: Derived from love
Amina   Swahili: Trustworthy
Aminah   Arabic: Honest
Amira   NA: Queen
Amy   Latin: Beloved Also Amie
Ana : A Spanish form of Anna
Anaka   Ibo: To share
Anastasia   Greek: Z (Αναστασια) Resurrection Also Annastasia, Anastashia
Angela   Greek: (Αγγελος)Messenger; the feminine form of Angel
Angelica   Latin: Like and angel Also Angelika, Angelique
Angelois : A blend of Angela and Lois
Angleine : This form of Angela
Anissa   Greek: (Ανισα) Unequal
Anita   Spanish: A diminutive for Ann
Ann : The English version of the Hannah
Annaritta : My love Pet name
Annette : A French form of Ann Also Annetta

Annis   Greek: Whole, complete

Annulette   : Of French origin

Anona   Latin: The Roman goddess of the harvest Also Anonna

Antigon   Greek: Of greek mythology

Antoinette   Latin: Priceless; a feminine version of Anthony

Apia   Caribbean: A popular last name in the Caribbean; Appia

April   Latin: Opening up or born in April

Araba   Akan: Born on Tuesday

Arberta   : African-American invented

Arcadia   Greek: Happiness Also Arcada

Ardella   Latin: Ardent with enthusiasm

Arenia   Greek origin

Areta   Greek: Virtue Also Aretha

Ariadne   Greek: Chaste Also Ariana, Arriana

Arlene   Latin: Strong, womanly Also Arlyn

Arnell   : The feminine form of Arnold

Arsula   : African American invented

Artemis   : From the Greek mythology

Asa   NA: Life is given

Asabi   Yoruba: One of high birth

Asesimba   Swahili: Born noble

Asha   Swahili: : Life in wealth

Ashanta   : A variation of Ashanti

Asma   Arabic: Precious

Asmahani   Swahili: exalted

Asumini   Swahili: jasmine

Athena   Greek: (Αθηνα) Wisdom Also Athenia

Atiya   Swahili: gift

Atta   Akan: Twin

Atwooki   Uganda: She is beautiful

Audreen   : A form of Audrey

Audrey   English: Noble strength Also Audra, Audre

Augusta   Latin: Exalted; feminine version of Augustus

Aurelia   Latin: Golden

Aurora   Latin: Roman goddess of dawn

Autree   : A variation of Audrey

Ava   Hebrew: Like a bird

Avis   Latin: A bird

Awali   Ibo: Joyful

Awena   Swahili: gentle

Ayanna   Ibo: One who takes care of the father

Ayanna   Swahili: She is a beautiful flower

Ayo   Yoruba: Joy

Ayobami   Yoruba: I am blessed with joy

Ayobunni   Yoruba: Joy

Ayofemi   Yoruba: Joy

Ayoola   Ibo:Celebration

Aza   Swahili: powerful

Azalia   Native American origin Also Azie

Azania   Native American origin

Azariah   Hebrew: Whom God helps

Aziza   NA: Dignity

Aziza   Swahili: precious

Aziza   Swahili: Precious

Azubu   Ibo: Keeper

B

Baaba   Akan: Born on Thursday

Baba   Fante: Born on Thursday

Babette   : A diminutive for Barbara

Babirye   Uganda: Elder twin sister

Baderinwa   Yoruba: Worthy of respect

Badriya   Swahili: moonlike

Bahati   Swahili: Luck

Bahatiya   Swahili: She brings luck

Bahiya   Swahili: Beautiful

Bakhitah   NA: Fortunate

Balenda   : Popular with free blacks of the 18th century

Barbar   Greek: (Βαρβαρος) Barbarian, foreign

Barke   Swahili: Blessings

Barnetta   African-American invented

Basha   Swahili: Act of God

Bashaam   Swahili: Rich

Bashira   Swahili: Predictor of good news

Basma   Swahili: Smile

Bathsheba   Biblical: Daughter of an oath

Batuuli   Swahili: Maiden

Baya   Swahili: Ugly

Bayo   Yoruba: Joy is found

Beata   Latin: Blessed happy one

Beatrice   Latin: She brings happiness

Bebi   Swahili: Baby

Becki   : A diminutive for Rebecca

Beda   English: Warrior maiden

Bedelia   Irish: Strength

Beduwa   Akan: The tenth born child

Bejide   Yoruba: Girl born during a rainstorm

Bela   Czech: White Also Belalisa Bellah

Belinda   Flemish: Beautiful

Belle   : A variation of Belessa

Belle   French: Beautiful Also Bell

Bemshi   Hindi: Let me in

Bena   Hebrew: Wise; a feminine form of Ben

Benita   Latin: Blessed

Bera   German: of the bear

Berdine   German: Bright maiden

Berit   Scandinavian: Magnificent

Bernadette   French: Courageous as a bear Feminine form of Bernard

Bernice   Latin: She who brings victory

Berta   : A variation of Bertha

Bertha   German: Bright

Bertie   A nickname for various names ending in bert

Bertina   German: Shining bright

Bess   Biblical: Consecrated to God Also Bessie, Bessy, Bessye

Beth   Hebrew: Short form for Elizabeth Betsy Betty

Beulah   Hebrew: She who is to be married

Beverly   English: Dweller at the beaver meadow

Bia   Swahili: Home

Bianca   Italian: White

Biddy   Flemish: form of Buddy

Billie   English: Resolute, has willpower

Bilqisi   Swahili: Queen of Sheba

Bimbaya   Swahili: Ugly lady

Bimkubwa   Swahili: A great lady

Bimkubwa   Swahili: Older lady

Binah   Senegal: Coin

Bindogo   Swahili: Young lady

Birdie   English: Little birdlike one Also Birdia

Birungi   Uganda: Nice

Blanche   French: The fair, white one

Blossom   English: Fresh
Bobbie   : Pet form of Roberta
Bolade   Yoruba: Honor arrives
Bolanile   Yoruba: She is the wealth of her home
Bonelle   African-American invented
Boniswa   SA: That which has been unveiled
Bonita   Spanish: Pretty
Bonnie   Scottish: The good one, fair of face
Brandy is popular with by black parents
Brenda   German: Firebrand
Brenna   Irish: Raven maid
Bria   Ethopia: Sunny
Briana   : Ferminine form of Brian Also Briane
Bridget   Irish: Strong, protective power
Brie   French: Cheese producing reggion
Brunella   French: Little one with brown hair
Bunmi   Yoruba: My gift
Bupe   Nyakyusa: Hospitality
Burdelle   : African-American invented
Buseje   Yao: Ask me

C

Calandra   Greek: (Καλανδρα) Lark
Calina   Greek: See Kalina
Camelia   American: A flower
Camille   Latin: Young ceremonial attendant
Candace   Latin: Glitter, glowing white
Canzata   Mexico: Stand
Cara   Latin: Darling
Caress   French: Dear one
Carina   Italian: Dear little one
Carita   Latin: Beloved
Carla   : The feminine form of Carl
Carlene : Variation of Carla, Carleta This variation of Carla
Carlotta   : Used by African-Americans; pet name for Carla
Carmen   Latin: A song
Carnella   : African-American invented
Carol   Latin: From Carola; strong and feminine. Form of Charles
Casey   Irish: Watchful

Cassandra   Greek origin; a prophet in the Greek mythology
Catherine   Greek: (Καθερινη) Pure one; Catherina, Kathy
Cecilia   Latin; Blind, dimly sighted one; a feminine form of Cecil
Cecily   : A form of Cecilia Also Cicely
Cedrice   Greek: (Κενδριζω) Agood weaver
Celeste   Latin: Heavenly Also Celina, Celestine
Celina   Greek: (Σελινη) The Moon
Chalina   Spanish: A diminutive for Rosa
Chana   Hebrew: A variant of Hannah
Chandelle   French: Candle Also Candel
Chandra   Hindi: Of the moon
Chanel   French: Canal
Chante   : A dimunitive of Shanty
Chantel   French: Singer Also Chantell
Chaonaine   Ogoni: She has seen me
Charcey   : African American form for Charles
Charity   Latin: Benevolent
Charla   : A feminine form of Charles
Charlayne   : A feminine form of Charles
Charlene   : A feminine form of Charles
Charlotte   French: Womanly, petite Also Carlotta, Charlotta
Charmaine   French: Fruitful orchard Also Charmayne
Chelsea   English: Landing place on the river
Chenzira   SA: Born to the road
Cherry   Englsih: A diminutive for Charity
Cheryl   : Caribbean favorite for the ferminine Also Cheryll, Sheryl
Chessa   : Slavic At peace Also Chesna
Chewa   SA: A strong tribe
Cheyenne   Native American: Believe to be a dimunitive of John
Chia   Philipino: Beautiful flower
Chiku   Swahili: Charterer
child   Adebomi Yoruba: The crown covers my nakedness
Chimodu   Ibo: God the protector
Chimwala   Yao: A stone
Chinua   Ibo: God's own
Chinyere   Ibo: God's gift is the name of the baby on the cover
Chioma   Ibo: The good
Chioneso   SA: Guiding light
Chiosa   Ibo: God of all
Chipo   SA: Great gift

Chipo   Shona: A gift
Chloe   Greek: (Κλεο) Short form for Cleopatra
Chotsani Yao: Take away
Christie : Diminutive for Christine Also Christy, Christi
Christine   French: A feminine form of Christian
Cindy   : Diminutive for Cynthia Also Cindi
Cissie or CC, A pet form of Cecily
Clara   Latin: Brilliant
Clarice   French: Little brilliant one
Claudette : A variation of Claudia
Claudia   Latin: Lame; a feminine form of Claude
Claudine A variation of Claudia
Clearita African-American invented
Clementia   Latin: Calm, merciful
Clementine the feminine form of Clement
Colette   French: Victorious army
Colleen   Irish: Maiden
Comfort   French: To comfort
Concordia   Latin: Harmony
Conney : Pet form for Cornelia Also Connie
Constance   Latin: Steadfastness
Cora   Greek: (Κορη) Maiden Also Coretta
Coral   Latin: A semiprecious growth under the sea
Cordelia   Welsh: A Ghanal from the sea
Corliss   English: Good-hearted, carefree
Courtney   English: Court dweller
Crecia Short form of Lucretia
Cressa   Greek: (Χρισσα) Christian; Chrissa, Crissina
Creta. Greek: Κρητη) Durable, hails from Crete
Crola   Spanish: Dark-skinned one
Crystal   Latin: Beautiful
Cynthia   Greek: The moon
Cyrena : Name from the greek mythology
Cyrilla : Form of Cyril

D
Dada   Yoruba: She has curly hair
Dahlia   Swedish: Valley
Daisy   English: Eye of the day Also Dessie
Dakota   : Native American: Friendly ally

Dale   English: From the valley

Dalila   Swahili: Gentle

Dalili   Swahili: Signs

Dallas   Scottish: From Dallas, a village in Scotland

Dana   English: From Denmark

Danette   A feminine version of Daniel Also Danita

Danielle   Biblical: God is my judge; a feminine version of Daniel

Daphne   Greek: (Δαφνη) Flower Also Daphna

Dara   Hebrew: House of wisdom

Darcy   Irish: Dark Also Darcie, Darcey

Darice   Greek: (Δαρηση) Wealth; a feminine form of Darius

Darlene   English: Dearly beloved, darling

Dasia   Hebrew: God's law

Davette   A feminine form David

Dawning   English: The first light of the morning sun. Dawn for female

Daya   Hebrew: Resemblance with a bird

Dayo   Yoruba: Joy arrives

Dazell   Derived from Dazle Praise name of AA Invention Also Dazelle

De Vera   Of Spanish origin

Dearie   English: Darling Pet name

Debbie   A diminutive for Deborah

Deborah   Hebrew: To speak kingly

Debra   A variation of Deborah

Decca   Greek: (Δεκα) Tenth Also Deka

Decia   Latin: Tenth

Deidre   Irish: Compassion

Dejeurnetta   Impeccable charater. Derived from the Ibo: De ije ome ta

Delena   Greek: ΔιηλΗνα) Shy Also Delita, pet form

Delfina   Greek: Delphi

Delia   Greek: visible

Delilah   Biblical: Gentle

Della   Pet form of Adele

Delora   Latin: From the seashore Also Delois, Delores

Delpha   Greek: Dolphin

Delta   Greek: (Δελτα) Fourth alphabet

Demetra   Greek: (Δημητρα) Fertile˙

Dena   English: From the valley; a feminine version of Dean

Denise   Greek: From Dionysus, Greek God of wine

Deonisia   A feminine version of Dennis

Desiree   French: Greatly desired; Desery, Desiree

Devona   English: From Devonshire
Devora   A variation of deborah
Dewanda   AA invention
Dewilda   AA invention
Diamond   Greek: (Διαμαντι) Diamond, Brilliant
Diana   English: Divine Also Dianna
Diane   French: Divine
Dikeledi   Tswana: Tears
Dinah   Hebrew: Judged and avenged
Dinora   Spanish: A form of Dinah
Divina   Hebrew: Greatly loved Also Devinia, Davina
Dixie, Dixon   English origin
Djuana   Cameroon: Joanna
Do   Ghana: First child following twins
Dofi   Ghana: Second child following twins
Dolly   A short form of Dorothy
Dolores   Spanish: A favored name honoring the Virgin Mary
Dominique   Latin: Belonging to the Lord
Donella   Irish: Dark-haired girl
Donna   Italian: Lady; a feminine form of the Latin word for Lord
Dora   Greek: (Δωρα) A gift
Dorcas   Greek: (Δωρεας) Charity
Doreen   French: Gilded
Doretha   Greek: Gift of God Also Dorethae
Doris   Greek: Bountiful, from the sea
Dorothy   Greek: (Δωροθεα) Gift of God Also Dorothea
Doto   Zaramo: Second born of twins
Douye   Ibo: We got what we sought
Dovie   Derived from the bird Dove
Duku   Akan: The eleventh born
Dulcie   Latin: Sweet one
Dyese   CA: This is my fortune
Dziko   Nguni: The world

E
Earlene   German: Shield; a feminine form of Earl Also Earlene, Early
Earmine   Ethiopia: To God be   Originated from Yarmin
Eartha   English: The earth Earthalee
Easter   English: Born at Easter time
Ebi   Ibo: Good thought

Ebony   English: Black; the name of a rare type of black wood
Ebun   Yoruba: A gift
Edana   Irish: Ardent
Edeline   German: Of good cheer
Edina   Englsih: prospering and happy
Edisa   Of AA invention
Edith   English: Rich gift
Edlyn   English: Little princess
Edmonda   English: Prosperous. (F) for Edmund; Edmunda, Edmonia
Edna   Hebrew: Rejuvenation Also Ednah
Edra   Hebrew: Powerful
Edria   English: Powerful, prosperous Also Edrea
Edris   English: Wealthy, powerful; a feminine version of Edric
Edwina   Englsih: Wealthy friend; a feminine version of Edwin
Effie   Greek: Intelligent short form of Iffigenia
Efia   Fante: Born on Friday
Efie   Akan: Born on Friday
Efua   Akan: Born on Friday
Eileen   Irish: Brilliant,
Eirene   Greek: (Αντιγονη) Another form of Irene: Peace
Ekuwa   Akan: Born on Wednesday
El-Jamah   NA: Paradise
Elaine   French: Bright light; a form of Helen
Elana   Hebrew: A tree Also Ilana
Eldora   Spanish: Gift of the sun
Eldra   Of AA invention Rarely used today
Elektra   Greek: Electric Also Electra
Eleni   Greek: (Ελενη) Light
Elise   French: Pledged to God; a short form of Elizabeth Also Elisa, Elissa
Elizabeth   Hebrew: Consecrated to God Also Elisabeth, Liz short form
Ellice   Greek: Jehovah is God; a feminine form of Elias
Elma   German: God's protection Also Elmetta
Elmina   African-American invented A variation of Elma
Elmira   English: Popular
Elva   Spanish Form of Elvira
Elvina   English: Noble friend
Emily   Latin: Industrious
Enrique   Spanish: One who rules his household
Enyonyam   Ghana: It is good for me
Era   Greek: (Ερα) Centurious

Erica   Scandinavian: Rules forever Also Erika, Ericka
Eshe   Swahili: Life
Esi   Fante: Born on Sunday
Esther   Persian: Star
Etan   Shekiri: God's love never ceases
Ethel   German: Noble
Eugenia   Greek: (Ευγενια) Polite; a feminine form of Eugene
Eunice   Greek: Joyful, victorious conqueror
Eurania   Greek (Ουρανια): Heavenly
Eva   Hebrew: The Living one Also Eve, Evie, Evita
Evangeline   Greek (Ευαγγελια): Good news
Evette   French: A variation of Yvette; a diminutive for Yvonne
Evona, Evana   Popular names from biblical sources
Evonne   French: Archer's bow; a variation of Yvonne Also Eyvonne

F
Fabayo   Yoruba: A lucky birth is joy
Fadilah   Arabic: Virtue
 Fadwa   Arabic: Sacrifice
Faith   Latin: Ever true
Faizah   Arabic: Victorious
Fari   Wolof: The queen
Faridah   Arabic: Unique
Farihah   Arabic: Joyful
Fashola   Yoruba: God's blessing
Fatia   NA: Daughter of the prophet
Fatima   Arabic: Daughter of the prophet
Fatima   Arabic: Fatima was a daughter of the prophet Muhammad
Fatimah   NA: Daughter of the prophet
Fatinah   Arabic: Captivating
Fatuma   Swahili: Daughter of the prophet
Fay   French: Fairy English: Related to faith Also Faye, Fayette
Fayola   Yoruba: Good fortune walks with honor
Felicia   Latin: Lucky
Femi   Yoruba: Love me
Fennella   Irish: White shoulder
Fifi   French: A diminutive for Josephine
Flemmie   A form of Flemming
Flora   Latin: Flower Florastine, A variation of Flora Also Florine
Fola   Yoruba: Honor Folade Yoruba: Honor arrives

Folam   Yoruba: Respect and honor me
Folashade   Yoruba: Honor gets a crown
Folayan   Yoruba: Walk in dignity
Foluke   Yoruba: Placed in God's care
Fontanne   French: Spring, fountain Fontana A variation of Fontanna
Fortune   Latin: Good fate, good destiny
Fotoula   Greek (Φοτουλα) Shinning Light From the word Phos: Light
Frances   Latin: From France; a feminine form of Francis Also Frankie
Freda   German: Peaceful
Fuju   Swahili: Born after parents' separation
Fukayna   Arabic: Studious

G

Gabriella   Italian: God is my strength
Gail   English: Joyful, lively one Also Gale
Galina   A Russian form of Helen
Gamer   NA: Moon
Gaye   French: Bright Also Gayline Gayleen, Gail
Geneva   French: The tree
Georgia   Greek (Γεωργος): A farmer; a feminine version of George
Geraldine   German: Rules by the spear
Germaine   German: From Germany
Geronda   Greek: Old
Gertrude   German: Spear maiden
Ghadah   Arabic: Beautiful
Ghanah   WA: Born on (Sunday)
Ghayda Arabic: Young and delicate
Ghika   Ibo: God is the greatest
Gilda   English: Golden one
Gina   A short form for Regina
Ginger   English: Nickname for Virginia
Gladys   Latin: Lame
Glenda   Welsh: Fair and good Also Glinda
Gloria   Latin: Glory
Golda   English: Gold
Goldie   Popular diminutive for Golda
Goumba   Wolof: Blind
Grace   Latin Graceful, attractive one
Gus   Ibo: short form for Ngozi
Gwendolyn   Welsh: Fair

H

Habibah   Arabic: Beloved
Haddie   Greek: (Χαιδευω) Caress
Hadiah   NA: Quiet and calm
Hadiya   Swahili: A gift from God
Hadiyah   Arabic: Guide to righteousness
Hadiyyah   Arabic: Gift
Hadley   Englsih: From the field of heather
Hagar   Biblical: Forsaken stranger
Haley   Irish: Ingenious
Halima   Swahili: Gentle
Halle   A form of Holly
Hana   Arabic: Happiness
Hanifah   Arabic: True believer
Haniyyah   Arabic: Happy
Hannah   Biblical: Graceful
Haqikah   Arabic: Truthful
Harlene   Englsih: From the meadow of the hares
Harmony   Latin: Harmonious, fitting
Harriet   French: Ruler of the estate
Hasanati   Swahili: Good
Hasina   Swahili: Good
Hasna   Arabic: Beautiful
Havenia   A diferent form of Haven
Hawa   Swahili: Longing
Hayfa   Arabic: Slender, beautiful body
Hazel   Englsih: The hazelnut tree Hazeline A variation of Hazel
Heather   Englsih: A flower name referring to the heather
Hedda   German: Strife in battle
Hedy   Greek: Sweet
Heidi   German: Noble and cheerful
Helga   Scandinavian: Holy one
Hellena   This variant of Helen
Heloise   French: Famous in war; a form of Louise
Henrietta   German: Ruler of the house
Hermione   Greek: Earthly
Hermosa   Spanish: Beautiful
Hester   Greek: A star; a form of Esther
Hilary   Greek: Cheerful Also Hillary
Hilda   German: Battle maid

Holly   Englsih: Holly tree, holy
Honey   English: Sweet one
Honora   Latin: Honorable
Hope   English: Also Hoppie
Hyacinth   Greek: The purple Hyacinth flower

I
Ianthe   Greek: Violet flower
Ida   German: Industrious
Idalette   A A invention
Idelle   Irish: Bountiful
Idina   English: From Edinburgh
Iesha   Yoruba: Derived from IIesha
Ife   Yoruba: Love
Ifeakanwa   Ibo: A child iss the best
Ifeanyichuckwu   Ibo: Nothing is impossible with God
Ifella   Ibo: Unforgettable
Ifetayo   Yoruba: Love brings happiness
Ifoma   Ibo: Goodluck Also Ifeoma
Ige   Yoruba: Delivered feetfirst
Ikella   Ibo: Lasting Strenght
Ilana   Hebrew: Tree
Ilene   Irish: Light; a variation of Eileen; Helen
Ilia   Greek: Derived from Iliazos; of the light
Ilsa   German: Noble maiden
Imani   Swahili: Leader
Ina   Latin: Mother
Inambura   SA: Rain mother
Inda   Believed to originated India
Inell   AA invention
Inez   Spanish: Pure
Iola   Greek: Violet Short form of many greek names
Iona   Greek: Violet Also Ionia
Irene   Greek: (Ειρηνη) Peace
Iris   Greek: The rainbow, a flower
Irma   German: Noble one
Irvette   English: Sea friend; a feminine version of Irving
Isabel   Spanish: Consecrated to God Also Isabelle, Isabella
Isadora   Greek: Gift of Isis, the principal goddess of ancient Egypt
Isoke   Benin: A good gift from God

Ivana   This Slavic feminine of John
Iverem   Tiv: Blessing
Ivory   Latin: Precious substance
Ivy   English: A vine
Izegbe   Benin: Long expected child
Izell   Turkish: The one; Izetta
Izola   Central Region: A Rich plant

J

J. English: A precious gem
Jacqueline   French: Protect The French form of James
Jada   Arabia: Mountainous place
Jaha   Swahili: Dignity
Jala   Arabic: Lucid
Jamaica   A Caribbean Island
Jamie   Scottish: A diminutive for James
Jamila   Swahili: Beautiful
Jamila   Arabic: Beautiful
Jamilah   Arabic: Beautiful
Jan   Hebrew: The Lord is gracious; (F) form of John; Jana, Jane
Janet   A form of Jane Also Janel, Janie, Janice A variation of Jane
Japera   Shona: It is done
Jaribu   Swahili: One who tries
Jasmine   Arabic: A flower
Jean   Latin: Popular with French speaking African countries; Jeannine
Jelena   A Russian variation of Helen
Jemima   Hebrew: Little dove
Jemine   Shekiri: God's wish Also Jemi, as a pet forrm
Jendayi   Shona: Give thanks
Jenesa   AA variation for Genesis
Jennifer   Welsh: White
Jessica   Hebrew: Wealthy AlsoJessie
Jetaime   French: I love you
Jetta   German: Fast
Jill   Latin: Youthful From Gillian
Jimelle   A feminine variation of Jim
Joan   Hebrew: The Lord is gracious
Jocelyn   AA invention from Joyce and Lynn
Jodelle   A pet form of Joel Also Jodie, Jody
Joella   Hebrew: Jehovah is the Lord

Johanna   Latin: God is gracious
Joie   Portuguese: A form of Joseph
Jokha   Swahili: The robe of royalty
Jolomi   Shekiri: The Lord has settled me
Josephine   Hebrew: She will add
Joy   Engish: Joyful
Joyce   Latin: Joyous
Juanita   Spanish: God is gracious
Jubemi   Shekiri: The Lord has answered my prayers
Judith   Hebrew: Jewess
Julia   Latin: Youthful Also Julet
Jumanah   Arabic: Silver pearl
Jumapili   Mwera: Born on Sunday
June   Latin: Sixth month
Junetta   of June
Justine   French: Fair, upright Also Justina

K
Kadija   NA: Blessed one Also Khadijah
Kafi   CA: Serene
Kai   Hawaiian: Seawater
Kaila   Hawaiian: A flower crown
Kaitlin   Irish: Catherine
Kakra   Fante: Youngest
Kala   Greek: Good
Kala   Hindu: Black
Kalani   Hawaiian: The sky chief
Kali   Sanskrit: Energy
Kalifa   Somali: Chaste, holy
Kalila   Arabic: Sweet heart, beloved
Kalina   Greek: (Καλινα) Good natured
Kalinda   Pet name for Linda
Kalisa   Greek: Pet form of Kali Also Kallie
Kamaria   Swahili: Beauty of the moon
Kamilah   Arabic: The perfect one
Kanika   Mwera: Black
Kara   Latin: Beloved, sweetheart
Karen   A Danish form of Catherine
Karma   A Hindu: Destiny
Kate   This diminutive for Catherine

Kathleen   An Irish form of Katherine
Katia   An unusual form of Kate
Katokwe   CA: Happiness is mine
Katou   Uganda: Small
Katy   A diminutive for Katherine
Kay   A nickname for Katherine or Karen
Kayla   Australian: A rodent that lives in mountainous areas
Kefiwe   Tswana: I receive grace
Kehinde   Yoruba: Younger
Keisha   AA Invented
Kelly   Irish: Battle maid
Kemba   CA: She is full of faith
Kerensa   Australia: Beloved
Kerry   Irish: Dark one Also Kerrie, Kerri, Keri
Kesi   Swahili: Born when father was in trouble
Keziah   Ancient origin
Khadijah   Arabic Name twin of prophet Muhammad's wife
Khalidah   Arabic: Immortal
Khalilah   Arabic Feminine version of Kamilah
Kia   AA invented
Kibibi   Swahili: Little
Kifimbo   Swahili: A very fragile baby
Kigongo   Cameroon: Born before twins
Kiiza   Cameroon: Born before twins
Kilolo   CA: Youth shines on her
Kim   A diminutive for Kimberley
Kimmie   A diminutive for Kimberley
Kinshasha   Capital city of Zaire
Kirsten   Scandinavian: A form of Christine
Kisaye   Uganda: Belonging to God
Kissa   Cameroon: Born after twins
Kissie   A diminutive for Kiss
Kitra   Hebrew: Crowned one
Kitty   A short form of Katherine
Kizuwanda   Zaramo: The last born
Kizzie   A diminutive for Keziah
Koma   Ghana: Belonging to the people AlsoKometa
Kristen   A form of Christine Also Kristina, Kristy, Christine
Kukua   Fante: Born on Wednesday
Kutu   NA: One of twins

Kweli   Ga: Believer

Kyeeniah   AA Invention, originated from Kenya

Kyla   A feminine form of Kyle

Kyra   Greek: (Κυρια) Lady; a title of respect

L

Lafiette   From Lafayette French roigin

Lahalia   AA Invented

Laini   Swahili: Sweet and gentle, soft

Lamya   Arabic: Dark-lipped

Lana   A form of Alana

Lara   Latin: In Roman mythology

Larissa   Greek: Cheerful

Latifah   Arabic: Gentle, kind Also Lateefah

Latiffah   African-American invented

LaToya   African-American invented

Latrice   Greek: (Λατρης) The believer

Laura   Latin: Laurel; a feminine form of Laurus Also Lauraine

Lauranell   A variation of Laura found among modern schoolgirls

Laureen   A variation of Laura Also Lauren, Laurina, Laurence, Loren

Lauretta   A variation of Laura

Laurice   A variation of Laura

Laveda   Latin: Purified, cleansed Also Lavella, Lavelle, Lavetta, Lavette

Laverne   Latin: Laverna, the Roman goddess of thieves and liars

Lavinia   Latin: Lady from Rome

Lavonia   A feminine form of Lavon

Layla   Swahili: She was born at night

Leah   Biblical: Weary

Leala   French: Loyal, faithful Also Layla

Leandra   Greek: lion man Feminine form of Leander

Leanna   Irish: Loving Also Leanne

Leila   Arabic: Dark as night, affectionate

Lekisha   Ga: Queen of the sea Also Leksha

Lemonia   Greek: (Λεμονι) Sweet scent Also Lemona

Lena   Latin: She who allures

Lenora   Greek:(Λενορα) Bright, shining light; a form of Eleanor

Leona   Greek: (Λεονταρι) Lionness; (F) form of Leon; Leonia Leontine

LeShiryl   AA Invention

Lessie   A dimunitive of Lesslie

Lestine   Believed to be derived from Celetine Also Lesta

Leta Latin: Glad
Letha Greek: Forgetfulness Also Lethea, Lethia
Levana Latin: to rise
Levina English: A flash of bright light Also Levinia
Levisa AA invention
Levita AA invention Popular in Florida
Lexie Believed to be coined out of Lexington
Liana French: To wrap around
Lila A variation of Leila Also Liela, Liella Lillian
Lily Latin: A flower; Adelina, Angelina, Emelina, Carolina
Lina Arabic: Tender
Linda SA: Goodness awaits me
Linda Spanish: Pretty
Lindiwe SA: Moment of rapture
Lindsay Scottish: From the linden tree grove
Linette A variation of Lynette Also Linnetta
Lisa Hebrew: Pledged to God
Litha Greek: (Λιθη) Stone
Liza A diminutive for Elizabeth Lizzelle Also Lizzell
Lobertha AA invented
Lois AA variation of Louise
Lola A diminutive for Dolores
Lolli Wolof: Fall
Lora A pet form of Laura
Lorena Variations of Laura
Loretta AA variation of Laura
Lori A variation of Laura Also Loris, Loriel
Lorna Scottish: From the place name Lorn
Lorraine French: From Lorraine, an eastern province in France
Lottie French: Little woman
Lou This short form of Louise
Louise French: Famous warrior; a feminine form of Louis
Lovie Also Lovey
Lozetta Lozetta is AA inventedvariation of Loretta
Luberta African-American invented
Lucena A form of Lucia
Lucetta A form of Lucy
Lucia Latin: Light
Lucille French: Light Also Lucilla
Lucinda Latin: Light

Lucretai   Latin: Wealth
Lucy   Latin: Wealth
Luetta   A variation of Lou
Lulu   Swahili: A pearl
Lumengo   CA: A flower of the people
Lumusi   Ghana: Born facedown
Lydia   Greek: Meaning unknown
Lynette   Welsh: Icon

M
Maanan   Akan: Fourth born child
Mabel   Latin: Lovable
Macey   AA invention
Madeline   Hebrew: Magnificent Also Magda
Madena   Italia: Resembling Madonna
Madihah   Arabic: Praiseworthy
Madonna   Latin: my lady
Madora   A form of Medea
Mae   Also May
Mafaune   Bachopi: Soil
Magano   SA: Gift
Magena   Hebrew: Melody
Maggy   A diminutive for Margaret
Magnolia   French: The magnolia tree
Maha   NA: Beautiful eyes
Mahalia   Swahili: Hostile space, The desert
Maia   Greek: (Μητερα)Mother
Maida   English: A maiden
Maizah   Arabic: Discerning rains
Majesta   Latin: Dignity, majesty
Majidah   Arabic: Glorious
Malak   Arabic: Angel
Maliaka   Swahili: Queen Also Malaika
Malinda   Cantonia: Gentle
Maliqua   Derived from the Arabic name Maliq
Malissa   A variation of Melissa
Mama   Fante: Born on Saturday
Mande   Uganda: First day
Mandisa   Xhosa: Sweet
Mansa   Akan: Third born child

Mara   Hebrew: Bitter
Maram   Arabic: Aspiration
Marcella   Latin: Of the plaanet Mars
Marcenia   A variation of Marcia
Marcia   Latin: Warlike; a feminine form of Mark
Margaret   Greek: (Μαργαριταρι) A pearl
Marilyn   A frequently employed variation of Mary
Marion   French: A diminutive for Marie
Maris   Latin: Star of the sea
Marita   Latin: Married woman
Marjani   Swahili: Named for the beautiful coral
Marjoe   A combination of Mary and Joe
Marjorie   A variation of Margaret
Marla   A form of Marlene
Marlee   A combination of Mary and Lee
Marlene   A blend of Mary and Magdalene
Marsha   A form of Marcia
Marta   A variation of Martha
Martha   Biblical: Lady Also Martella, Martelle, Martina
Marva   Latin: Wonderful
Mary   Maria Popular name for females
Masani   Cameroon: Has gap between teeth
Masika   Swahili: Born during the season
Matilda   German: Mighty in battle
Matoka   Kenya: My favorite
Mattiwilda   Swahili: Matilda
Maureen   Irish: Little Mary
Mauve   Latin: Violet
Mavis   A short form for Marvellous
Mawakana   CA: I yield to the ancestors
Mawusi   Ghana: In the hands of God
Maxine   Latin: Greatest Also Maxene
May   Latin: Great one
May   Greek: Mother
Maya   A variation of Maia
Mayola   A compound name derived from May and Ola
Mbafor   Ibo: Home of major market place
Mbagun   NA: One of twins
Mbeke   Ibo: Born on the third market day
Medea   Greek: (Μηδεια) Ruling In Greek myth

Medora   English: Mother's gift
Melanie   Greek: (Μελανι) Black, of a dark complexion
Melba   AA invention
Melia   Greek: (Μιλια) Forunner Also Milia
Melina   Greek: (Μελι) Honey Also Melinda
Melissa   Greek: (Μελισσα) Honey bee
Melody   Greek: (Μελοδια) Song, beautiful music
Melvina   Irish: Chief
Mena   Greek: For me
Mendora   Another Puckett gem
Mercedes   Spanish: Merciful, compassionate
Meredith   Welsh: Magnificent lady
Meta   A diminutive for Margaret
Mia   Italian: My
Michaela   Ferminine form of Michael
Michelle   Biblical: Like unto the Lord
Migozo   CA: She is ernest
Mikki   A popular pet name for Michelle
Milagron   Spanish: Miraculous
Mildred   English: Gentle strength Also Milly
Mimi   A short form of Mildred
Mineola   Italian source
Minerva   Latin: The thinking one
Minnie   A diminutive for Mineola
Mirabelle   Latin: Wonderful
Miranda   Latin: Admirable
Miriam   Hedrew: Miriam
Missy   A pet form of Melissa
Mitzi   A German pet form of Maria
Mkiwa   Swahili: Orphaned
Modelia   A paraise name for a classy girl Of AA invention
Modupe   Yoruba: I am grateful
Mogbeyi   Shekiri: This one is my joy
Moisha   African American invented
Mona   NA: A great surprise
Mona   Irish: Aristocratic
Monica   Of Spanish origin
Monifa   Yoruba: I have luck
Montsho   Tswana: Black
Morena   Spanish: Brown, brown-haired

Mosi   Swahili: The first born
Mozelle Hebrew: Savior; a female form of Moses
Mpho   Tswana: Gift
Msiba   Swahili: Born during mourning
Mudiwa Shona: Beloved
Mulekwa   Uganda: Child born out of wedlock
Mumbejja   Uganda: Princess
Muna   Arabic: Wish
Muriel   Irish: Shining sea
Muteteli   Rwanda: Dainty
Muzaana   Uganda: The wife of a princess
Mwaka   Ibo: A child is the best blessing
Mwanjaa   Zaramo: Born during a feminine
Mwasaa   Swahili: Born on time
Myra   Spanish: Sweet smelling oil
Myrlie   A variation of Myrtle
Myrtle   English: A dark green bush

N
Naadu   Ga: One from the Sempeh region
Nabirye   Cameroon: Mother
Nabulungi   Cameroon: Beautiful one
Nabwire   Uganda: Born during the night
Nada   Arabic: Full of generosity
Nada   Russian: Hope
Nadia   NA: Time of promise
Nadine   French: Hope
Naeemah   Arabic: Benevolent
Nafisah   Arabic: Precious
Nailah   Arabic: She who will succeed
Najat   NA: Safe
Najibah   Arabic: Of noble birth
Najla   Arabic: Wide eyes
Nakampi   Uganda: Short
Nalongo   Cameroon: This is a Mother of twins
Namalwa   Uganda: Born of twins
Nan   Hebrew: Grace; a pet form of Hannah
Nanetta   Spanish pet name for Nancy
Nanyamka   Ghana: God's gift
Naomi   Biblical: Sweet, pleasant

Narcissa　Greek Greek mythology
Nasiche　Uganda: Born during the time of locust
Natalie　Latin: Birthday of Our Lord
Natasha　Russian: Birthday of our Lord
Nathifa　Arabic: Clean
Nayfa　Swahili: Benefit
Nayla　Swahili: Gain
Nayo　Yoruba: We have joy
Naysun　Swahili: Dangling seedless grapes
Nazarie　Nazlee, Nazarine, Nazrinie
Ndidi　Ibo: Patience
Neala　Irish: Champion; a feminine form of Neal
Neda　Englsih: A sanctuary
Neema　Swahili: Born during the rainy season
Neema　Swahili: Bounty
Nefertia　A variation of Nefertari, queen of Egypt
Nefira　Egypt: Ferry
Negina　Hebrew: Melody
Neimat　NA: Pleasant
Nelka　Ibo: A variation of Nnekka
Nell　Diminutive for Eleanor
Nelsena　A variation of Nelson
Neola　Greek: (Νεολαια) Juvenile
Nerita　Greek: (Νεριτα) A sea snail
Nerolia　Italian: The princess who discovered neroli oil
Nessa　Scandinavian: Rock projecting into the sea
Nesta　A pet form of Agnes
Neva　Spanish: Snowy
Newanna　Ibo: Compound name
Ngena　EA: Majestic in service
Ngina　EA: One who serves
Ngozi　Ibo: Blessing
Ngulinga　Ogoni: Weeping
Niara　Swahili: Of high purpose
Nicole　Greek: (Νικη) Victory of the all Nikki A nickname for Nicole
Nilia　Egypt: A different form of the river Nile
Nina　Swahili: Mother
Nina　Spanish: Girl
Nisri m　Swahili: Wild rose
Njemile　Yao: Upstanding

Nkechi   Ibo: Thisbelongs to God
Nkroma   Akan: The ninth child
Nneka   Ibo: Amother is the greatest
Nobanzi   Xhosa: Width
Nodie   Ibo: Igannodi You will stay
Noel   French: Christmas
Nola   Irish: White shoulders
Noleta   Latin: Unwilling
Nombeko   Xhosa: Respect
Nomble   Xhosa: Beautiful
Nomuula   Xhosa: Rain
Nona   Latin: Ninth Also Nonie
Nonyameko   Xhosa: Patience
Nora   Greek: Light; a short form of Eleanor or Honora
Norma   Latin: A rule, principle
Novia   Spanish: Girlfriend
Nsonwa   Akan: The seventh child
Ntosake   Zulu: She who walks with lions Also Ntozake
Nuebese   Benin: A wonderful child
Nuha   Swahili: Consoled
Nun   NA: Brightness
Nunu   Swahili: Extol
Nurami   NA: Brightness
Nuru   Swahili: Born in daylight
Nuru   Swahili: Light
Nuzha   Swahili: Pleasure
Nwakego   Ibo: A child is outstanding
Nyameke   Akan: Gift from God
Nydia   Latin: Nest

O
Obi   Ibo: A dimunitive for Obedience
Oboego   Ibo: The child that came with money
Octavia   Latin: Eight; a feminine version of Octavius
Odele   Ibo: Patience
Odelia   Hebrew: I will praise the Lord
Odessa   Greek: Long voyage
Odette   French: Wealthy
Oetha   Latin origin
Ola   Ibo: Wealth

Ola   Norwegian for Olga
Olabisi   Yoruba: Joy
Olabuni   Yoruba: We are rewarded with honor
Olaniyi   Yoruba: Glory
Olena   Ibo: Keeper of her father
Olenka   Ibo: Keeper of all the people
Olenza   Ibo: Keeper of the house
Olga   Russian: Holy
Olivetta   Italian: Form of Olive
Olivia   Latin: The olive tree
Olufemi   Yoruba: God loves me
Olufunke   Yoruba: A gift from God
Olufunmilayo   Yoruba: God gives joy
Oluremi   Yoruba: God consoles me
Olympia   Greek: From Mount Olympus Greek mythology
Oma   Ibo: Pet form of many Ibo names
Omagbemi   Shekiri: This child saved me Also Ogbemi
Omaone   Shekiri: I have a child
Omelia   A variation of Amelia
Omera   Ibo: The doer
Omizell   Ibo: The perfectionist
Omolara   Benin: Born during the night
Omorenomwara   Benin: This child will not suffer
Omorose   Benin: My beautiful child
Omosede   Benin: A child counts more than a king
Omosupe   Benin: A child is the most precious thing
Oneida   Native American: Long-awaited
Onella   Greek: Light
Oni   Benin: Desired
Onia   Ibo: Impossible
Onyeka   Ibo: Who is the greatest
Opal   Sanskrit: Precious stone
Ophelia   Greek: Wisdom Also Ophelia
Oprah   AA invention
Ora   Latin: Pray for us
Oralia   Latin: Golden; a form of Aurelia
Ordella   German: Spear
Orea   Greek: (Ορια) High grounds
Orela   Latin: A divine announcement
Orena   Greek: Far places

Oriana   Latin: Dawn, golden sunrise
Oseye   Benin: The happy one
Ozigbodi   Ghana: Patience
Ozora   Hebrew: Strength of the Lord

P
Palmira   Greek: Land of palm trees
Paloma   Spanish: A dove
Pam   A nickname for Pamela
Pandora   Greek: The all gifted one
Panthea   Greek: Home of all the gods
Panya   Swahili: Tiny like a mouse
Panyin   Fante: Elder of twins
Parthenia   Greek: Virginal
Pasca   Greek Easter
Pascale   French: Easter
Pat   A diminutive for Patricia
Patience   A popular vof the 1800
Patrice   A version of Patricia
Patricia   Latin: A woman of noble birth
Patty   A diminutive for Patricia
Paula   French: A feminine form of Paul Also Pauline
Peach   Popular as a pet name
Pearl   A precious name
Peggy   Originated from the Greek Margaret
Penelope   Greek: A weaver Also Penny
Petrina   Greek: Like a rock
Philantha   Greek:(Φιλανθη) Loves flowers
Phillis   Greek: A green branch
Philomena   Greek: The lover of songs
Phoebe   Greek: Radiant
Phyllis   Greek: A green branch
Pia   Latin: Pious
Pili   EA: The second child
Pili   Swahili: The second born child
Portia   Latin: An offer
Princess   English: Of royal birth
Princetta   Italian: A variation of Princess
Priscilla   Latin origin
Present ence   Latin origin

Pyrena   Greek: (Πυρινα)Fiery one

Q
Queen   Pet name

R
Rachel   Biblical: Ghana, female sheep
Radella   English: Elfin counselor
Radhiya   Swahili: Agreeable
Rae   A short form of Rache, Ray
Rahsheda   Arabic: Mature Also Rashidah
Raina   Latin: Queen; a variation of Regina
Raissa   French: Thinker, believer
Ramla   Swahili: Predicts the future
Ramona   Spanish: A mighty or wise guardian
Rana   Scandinavian The goddess of the sea
Randi   A feminine form of Randy
Ranita   Hebrew: joyous song
Raquel   A Spanish form of Rachel
Rashida   Swahili: Righ teous
Raven   English: A large black bird
Raziya   Swahili: Easy to get along with
Rebecca   Biblical: A firm bond
Regina   Latin: Queen
Rehema   Swahili: Of great compassion
Rena   Hebrew: Melody Also Reena
Renata   Latin: Born again
Rene   A diminutive for Irene
Renee   French: Reborn
Renita   Latin: A rebel
Rhea   Greek: Flowing
Rhoda   Greek: A rose
Rhona   Scandinavian: Rough isle
Rhonda   Welsh: Noisy waters
Ria   A variation of Victoria
Rita   Greek: A pearl
Riva   French: Riverbank
Robbie   Diminutive for Roberta
Roberta   English: Bright Also Robin
Rochelle   French: From the little rock

Rodella   Greek: Red
Rolanda   A feminine version of Roland
Rosa   Latin: A rose
Rosalind   Spanish: Beautiful rose
Rose   Latin: A flower name
Roseanne   A combination of Rose and Anne
Rosemary   Latin: Dew of the sea
Rowena   Welsh: Slender
Roxann   Persian: Brilliant one
Ruby   French: A precious gem
Rufaro   Shona: Happiness
Rukiya   Swahili: She rises on high
Ruth   Biblical: Beautiful

S
Saada   Swahili: Happiness
Saadiya   Swahili: Happy
Sabiha   Swahili: Beautiful
Sabina   Latin: From the Sabine
Sabrina   Latin: From the boundary line
Sada   Swahili: Help has come
Sade   Derived from the Yoruba name Olasade: Direct from God
Safa   Arabic: Clarity
Safaa   Swahili: Legibility
Safiya   Swahili: Clearminded, pure
Safiya   Swahili: Immaculate
Safiyyah   Arabic: Serene
Sage   Latin: Wise
Sagirah   Arabic: Little one
Sahara   Egypt: The rolling fields
Saida   Swahili: Happy
Sakina   Swahili: Peaceful
Salama   Swahili: Peace
Salamuu   Swahili: Safe
Salenia   Greek: Moon, Also a variation of Selina Salina, Selena
Salha   Swahili: Good
Salima or Salma   Swahili: Safe
Sally   Hebrew: Princess
Salma   Swahili: Safe
Salona   Derived from the biblical city of Salonika

Salwa   Swahili: Consolation

Samantha   Biblical: Asked of God

Samiha   Swahili: Generous

Samira   Swahili: Reconciler

Sandra   Greek: Helper of humankind Also Sandy

Sangeya   Shona: Hate men

Sanura   Swahili: Kitten

Sara (Sarah)   Joyful

Sara   NA: Gives pleasure

Sara   As a version of Sarah used by many chritian parents

Sarah   Biblical: Princess

Sauda   Swahili: Of a dark complexion

Saumu   Swahili: Fasting

Sauti   Swahili: Voice

Savory   AA invention

Sazidde   Uganda: Fourth day

Sebtuu   Swahili: Born on Saturday

Sekelaga   Nyakyusa: Rejoice

Sela   Hebrew: A rock

Selma   Arabic: Secure

Selma   German: Divine helmet

Semeni   Swahili: Speak

Serena   Latin: Tranquil

Serilda   German: Armored warrior maid

Serwa   Ghana: Royal woman

Shaba   NA: Morning has come

Shaba   Egypt: Of worsip

Shafiiqa   Swahili: Amiable

Shahrazad   Swahili: Princess

Shaina   Hebrew: Beautiful

Shakara   WA: Beautiful girl

Shakila   Swahili: well-rounded

Shamba   Swahili: Plantation

Shami   NA: Like the sun

Shamim   Swahili: Sweet scent

Shangwe   Swahili: Celebration

Shani   Swahili: Circumstance

Shannon   Irish: Ancient

Shantell   African American form

Sharifa   Swahili: Distinguished

Sharifa   Swahili: Noble
Sharon   Hebrew: Princess
Shawana   Swahili: Grace
Sheba   Hebrew: From queen Sheba
Shelley   English: Dweller in the meadow on the ledge
Shemeka   AA invented
Shenikwa   AA invented
Sherry   An American variant of Sharon
Sheryl   German: A variation of Cheryl
Shiminege   Tiv: Let us see the future in this purity
Shirley   English: From the bright meadow
Shoorai   Shona: Broom
Sibil   Greek: Prophetic
Sigele   Ogoni: Left
Sigolwide   Nyakyusa: My ways are straight
Silva   Latin: A maid for the woodlands
Simone   A feminine form of Simon
Sina   A form of mount Sinai
Singrid   Scandinavian: Beautiful counselor
Sirena   Greek: She who ensnares
Sisi   Fante: Born on a Sunday
Sit abua   NA: Her father loves her
Sojourner   Sojourner Truth left a lasting legacy in history
Sonya   Russian: Wisdom
Sophenia   A variation of Sophia
Sophia   Greek: Wisdom
Ssanyu   Uganda: Happiness
Stacey   Greek: Resurrection
Star   English: A brilliant heavenly body
Stella   Latin: Star
Stephanie   Greek: (Στεφανι) Crowned one; a feminine form of Stephen
Subria   Swahili: Patience rewarded
Sue   A diminutive for Susan
Suhailah   Arabic: Gentle
Sukutai   Shona: Squeeze
Sula   Propably from the greek name Tasula
Susan   Hebrew: Graceful lily Also Susanna, Susannah
Suubi   Uganda: Hope
Syandene   Nyakyusa: Punctual
Sylvania   Derived from Sylvia
Sylvia   Latin: Wood

T

Tabatha   Aramaic: A child of grace

Tabby   A nickname for Tabitha

Tabia   Swahili: Talented

Tacita   Latin: Silent

Taffy   Welsh: Beloved

Tahirah   Arabic: Pure

Tahiya   Swahili: Security

Taiwo   Yoruba: Firstborn of twins

Takiyah   Arabic: Righteous

Talha   Swahili: Easy life

Talitha   Aramaic: Damsel, a maiden of gentle or noble birth

Tamaa   Swahili: Greed

Tanabahi   Swahili: Be cautious

Taniesha   AA invention

Tanya   Russian: An abbreviated form of the Russian Tatiana

Tara   Irish: Tower

Tasha   Russian: Christmas

Tathmina   Swahili: High value

Tatiana   Russian origin

Tatu   Swahili: Three times

Tausi   Swahili: Peacock

Tawana   Also Twana, Twanna

Tawilu   Swahili: Tall

Taylora   Derived from Taylor

Taymura   Swahili: Guardian

Tefle   Swahili: Beginning

Teleza   Ogoni: Slippery

Telma   Greek: End

Teresa   Greek: Harvester Also Tess

Texanna   A lady from Tecas

Thalia   Greek: In bloom

Thelma   Coined from the Greek Thelema

Thema   Akan: Queen

Themba   Zulu: One to be trusted

Theodora   Greek: Given by God

Theola   Greek: Heavenly scent

Theophilla   Greek: God-loving Theofilos for men

Theresa   Greek: One who brings in the harvest

Thuwayba   Swahili: Small gift

Tia Spanish: Aunt Also Tiana, Tiara

Tiffany Greek: God appears

Tina Pet form of names such as Christina and Ernestina

Tiombe Zimbabwe: An achiever

Tisha Probably a variation of Letitia or Tricia

Titilayo Yoruba: Happiness is eternal

Toby Hebrew: The Lord is good

Toju Shekiri: God is all

Tonya A popular name in the Caribbean

Tosan Shekiri: God knows the best

Tracy A diminutive for Theresa

Tricia Latin: Aristocratic Also a pet name for Patricia

Tsoyo Shekiri: I'll take this joy

Tufaha Swahili: Apple

Tuhfa Swahili: gift

Tulimbwelu Nyakyusa: We are in the light of God

Tulinagwe Nyakyusa: God is with us

Tumpe Nyakyusa: Let us thank God for this child

Tumwebaze Uganda: Let us thank God for this child

Tuni Swahili: Tune

Tunu Swahili: Novelty

Turkiya Swahili: beautiful

Tyra Popular in the Caribbean

U

Uchechuckwu Ibo: God's guidance

Udele English: Wealthy

Udoka Ibo: Peace is better

Uliyemi Shekiri: Home suits me Also Yemi

Ulyssese This feminine form of Ulysses

Umayma Swahili: young mother

Umi Swahili: my mother

Umkultum Swahili: Prophet Muhammad's daughter

Umsa'ad Swahili: happy mother

Una Latin:The One

Undine Latin: Of the sea

Unguja Swahili: Zanzibar

Unis Also Eunice

Urania Greek: Heavenly

Urbi Benin: Princess

Ursula   Latin: Young female bear
Uwimana   Rwanda: Daughter of God

V
Valencia   Latin: Vigorous
Valentina   Latin: A feminine form of Valentino
Valentine   Latin: Healthy
Valerie   French: Strong
Valisha   AA invention
Valonia   Latin: From the valley
Valora   Latin: Valorous
Vana   This short form of Ivana
Vanessa   Popular with black parents in the 80s
Venus   Latin: Love and beauty
Veronica   Latin: True image
Vicky   A popular nickname for Victoria
Victoria   Latin: Victorious
Vinnette   A French nickname for Winfred
Vinney   An apparent diminutive for Vinnette
Viola   Latin: Violet
Violet   Latin: Purple
Vivian   Latin: Lively
Vynetta   Also Vinette

W
Waafa   Swahili: accomplishment
Wahiba   Swahili: gift
Walyam   Swahili: (William) protector
Wanda   German: The wanderer
Waseme   Swahili: Let them talk
Wendy   A diminutive for Wanda
Wesesa   Ewe: Careless
Whitney   English: White island
Wilda   English: Forest dweller
Willa   German: The desired
Winona   Native American: First daughter Also Wynona
Wudha   Uganda: Younger twin sister

X
Xanthe   Greek: Blondie

Xenia   Greek: Hospitable
Xhosa   SA: Give praises

Y
Yaa   Ghana: Born on Thursday
Yadikone   Wolof: You were here before
Yahimba   Tiv: There is no place like home
Yaminah   Arabic: Proper
Yasmin   Swahili: Jasmine
Yasmin   Arabic: Jasmine
Yathriba   Swahili: name for Madina
Ye   Ghana: Elder of twins
Yejide   Yoruba: She has her mother's face
Yetunde   Yoruba: Mother comes back
Yolanda   Greek: Violet flower
Yonah   Ferminine form of the name Jonah
Yumna   Swahili: good luck, happiness
Yusra   Swahili: ease
Yuuthar   Swahili: wealthy
Yvette   A diminutive for Yvonne
Yvonne   French: Archer Also Yevonne

Z
Zaafarani   Swahili: saffron
Zahra   Swahili: flower
Zahra ni   NA: Flower
Zaina   Swahili: beautiful
Zakiya   Swahili: Intelligent
Zalika   Swahili: Wellborn
Zandra   A variation of Sandra
Zara   Hebrew: Brightness, dawn Arabic: Princess
Zawadi   Swahili: A gift has come
Zelma   German: Under divine protection
Zenith   Latin origin
Zerlinda   Spanish: Beautiful dawn
Zesiro   Cameroon: The firstborn twin
Zia   Latin: Grain
Zodie   Coined from Zodiac
Zodie   Johnson was a well-known educator in Detroit
Zoe   Greek: Life; Zoi

Zola   Italian: A clump of earth
Zona   Greek: A girdle
Zora   Slavic: Dawn
Zuwena   Swahili: Good

NAMES FROM AROUND THE WORLD

ACHILLES
ADLER
ADWOA
AGATA
ALBERT
ALEX
ALICE
ALLAN
AMBROSE
ANDERSON
ANDREA
ANDREAS
ANDREW
ANDREY
ANN
ANN MARIE
ANNA
ANNESA
ANTHONY
ANTONIS
ANTWAN
APRIL
ARTHUR
ARTI
ATHANSIA
AUDREY
AYANNA
BADRU
BARBARA
BARHARA
BEBATH

BENJI
BERNADETTE
BERNADETTO
BERNARD
BESSIE
BETHANY
BEVERLY
BILL
BIRD
BOOTH
BORIS
BRIAN
BROTHER
BROWNE
BRYAN
BYRD
CAMANI
CARL
CARLA
CARLOS
CARMEN
CARMILA
CAROL
CAROLINA
CAROLINE
CARTREY
CATIUS
CATRINA
CERAR
CHARLES
CHERYL
CHESERETA
CHICHI

CHIOMA
CHRISTOPHER
CIANI
CIDA
CILA
CLARKE
CLIFFORD
CLIVE
CONSTANTINOS
CORA
COSTAS
CYNMIA
CYNTHIA
DANIEL
DANSETTE
DAPHNE
DARREN
DARRYL
DAVID
DAWN
DAWNE
DEBBIE
DEBORAH
DEJESUS
DEJU
DELLAND
DELORES
DELROY
DEMETRIS
DENISE
DESMOND
DESOTO

DEVITO	FORD	IYANLA
DIANA	FOSS	JAAQ
DIANNE	FRANCES	JACKLYN
DIMITRA	FRANCIS	JACKSON
DIMITRIOS	FRANCOIS	JACQUELINE
DIONNE	FRANK	JAH
DOMITTA	FRANK	JAHAAD
DONNA MARIE	FREDDY	JAM
DORA	FRITZ	JAMELA
DORETTA	FROZINE	JAMES
DOROTHEA	GEOFFREY	JANA
DOROTHY	GEORGE	JANICE
DOV	GERRARA	JAQUELINE
DREUWA	GIANNIS	JARETTE
DURU	GLORIA	JASPER
EDDIE	GLORIA	JAY
EDGAR	GOLDIMA	JEAN
EDNA	GORAN	JEAN
EDUARDO	GREENIDGE	JEANETTE
EEO	GREG	JEANNIE
ELEFTHERIA	GREGORY	JENNIFER
ELENI/HELEN	GUY	JEREMIAH
ELLA	HAITAFI	JIM
ELOTH	HARRY	JOAN
ELSA	HARRY	JOCELLA
EMAKA	HEATHER	JOHN
EMERY	HEKENI	JORR
EMMANUEL	HEKIO	JOS
ENRICO	HENNAN	JOSEPH
ERIC	HERNANDEZ	JUAN
ERMA	HOLLIS	JUANA
ERMALITA	HRISSI	JUANITA
EUSTACE	IESIA	JUDE
EVELYN	INDEY	JUDINO
FANNIE	INNOCENT	JULES
FAREIRA	IOANNA	KALU
FAY	IOANNIS	KANTE
FELIX	ISMENE	KAREN
FIDEL	IVAIS	KAREN
FLORIO	IVU	KATHLEEN
FORAASTENE	IYANDE	

KATHRYN
KEITH
KENNETH
KEREN
KETE
KEVIN
KOSTAS
KOUASSI
KRISTEN
KUMANI
KUMASI
KURZO
LAKIYA
LARONZ
LAURA
LAWRENCE
LEANDRO
LEFFERTA
LEOLIN
LEONARD
LETITIA
LEVI
LINDEN
LINDON
LISA
LLMA
LORI
LOUIRE
LOUIS
LOUISE
LU
LYDIA
LYNN
MAGGIE
MANUEL
MARCIA
MARCOS
MARGARET
MARGARITA
MARIA

MARIANO
MARIE
MARIO
MARK
MARLENE
MARTHA
MARY
MAWRICE
MCKENZIE
MELINDA
MERCADO
MEROTTA
MERRICK
META
MICHAEL
MICHELLE
MIMELE
MOHAMED
MOHINDAR
MOHNNDRO
MOLEFE
MOLEFI
MOZELL
MUSA
NANCY
NATHANIEL
NEASA
NELIE
NELIMAH
NELLIE
NEVEN
NGUYEN
NICHOLAS
NICK
NICOS
NIKI
NNANNA
NOEL
OCEANI
OMAR

ORLANDO
ORSON
OSONDU
OWEN
PAD
PANKAI
PARVEEN
PATRICIA
PATRICK
PAULINE
PERRY
PETER
PHIL
PIERRE
PLATON
POWELL
POWENI
RABI
RAHIM
RAMASATI
RAQUEL
RAYMOND
RAZA
REGINA
RENATA
REYNOLD
RHONA
RICARDO
RICE
RICHARDS
RIGELA
ROBERT
ROBINSON
RODAMI
RODNEY
ROHN
ROLAND
ROMMEL
RON
RONDA
RORHINA

ROSEMARY
ROSINA
ROSLYN
ROY
ROZANA
ROZAWA
RUPERT
RUSSETTA
RUTH
SAMANTHA
SANTOS
SCOT
SHARLEAN
SHARON
SHAWNA
SHERRIE
SHOELA
SHOLA
SHON
SILVA
SISLAM
SOCARIS
SOFIA
SOLO
SOMMIR
SOPHIA
SOUZA
STEPHANIE
STEPHEN
STEVAN
STEVE
STEVEN
SUBASHI
SUGARHILL
SUZANNE
SWOTHO
TEO
TERESA
TERRY
THELMA

THEMIS
THOS
TINA
TOM
TONIE
TONY
TONYA
TRACY
TSAWALA
TUNDE
UGO
UNA
URRON
URRUBO
VALERIE
VAN
VENETTA
VERNICE
VERONICA
VICTOR
VIVIAN
WADE
WILFRED
WILFREDO
WILLIAMS
WILLIE
WILMA
WURDROW
YERAC
YUOMEY
YUSUF
YVETTE
YVONNE
ZAKIR

ZANA
ZRICOS

ONWUCHEKWA NAMES

AJERE
ANASTASIA
BASSEY
BRAIMAH
CHIJIOKE
CHINYERE
CHRISTOPHER
COLLINS
ELEKWA
HASSAN
IKEKPERE
IVUOMA
MICHAEL
MOSES
NGBORO
NGOZI
NNENNAYA
OGO
SAMUEL
SOMTOCHUKU
TENJU
TOCHI

GREAT PEOPLE
OF COLOR

A. K. Davis
A. S. Thomas
A. T Walden
Aaron Douglas
Abby Lincoln
Abram Harris
Absalom Jones
Al Sharpton
Alain L. Locke
Albert Cleage
Albert Smith
Alexander Crummell
Alexander Payne
Alexandre Dumas
Alfred Cannon
Alice Elizabeth Catlett
Allan Rohan Crite
Alonzo di Pietro
Alvan Ikoku
Andrew Beard
Andrew Brimmer
Andrew Bryan
Andrew Young
Ann Petry
Anthony Overton
Antoine Dubuclet
Archibald Motley
Arna Bontemps
Arthur Clark
Arthur G Gaston
Arthur Mitchell
Arthur Schomburg
Arthur Sholes
Arthur Tappan
Asa G. Yancey
Augusta Savage
Augustus Tolton
B. F Howard
B. M. Ford
Baramendana Keita
Barbara Ann Teer
Barzillai Lew

Ben Hedge
Benjamin Banneker
Benjamin E Mays
Benjamin O. Davis, Jr.
Benjamin O. Davis, Sr.
Benjamin S. Turner
Benjamin Singleton
Benjamin Tucker
Bernard Goss
Bill Broonzy
Bill Cosby
Bill Matney
Bill Pickett
Binga Jesse
Blanche K Bruce
Bob Cole
Bob Teague
Booker T. Washington
Boyd Henry
Bunche Ralph
C. C. Spaulding
Caesar Brown
Camilla Williams
Campbell E. Simms
Carl Diton
Carmel Collins
Carol Brice
Carter Woodson
Cato Blackney
Cecil McBay
Chandler Owens
Charles Alston
Charles Gilpin
Charles Houston
Charles Maceo Thompson
Charles Nash
Charles Remond
Charles S. Johnson
Charles Sebree
Charles Turner
Charles Wesley
Charles White
Charles Young
Charley Patton
Charlie Parker

Chinua Achebe
Cicely Tyson
Clarence Brisco
Clarence Williams
Clarian Anderson
Claude Barnett
Claude McKay
Claudia McNeill
Constance Baker
Motley
Constance Webb
Cornish Samuel E
Countee Cullen
Crispus Attucks
Cuff Whittemore
Daddy Stovepipe
Daniel Coker
Daniel Hale Williams
David Blackwell
David P Ross
David Ruggles
Dean Dixon
Denmark Vesey
Diahann Carroll
Diana Sands
Dobbs Mattilda
Don L Iee
Don Mitchell
Dorothy Maynor
Douglas Turner Ward
Drew Charles
Du Bois William
Dunn Oscar
E. R Robinson
Earl Dickerson
Earl Hines
Ebenezer Bassett
Ed Bernard
Ed Bullins
Edmonia Lewis
Edouard Scott
Eduard Burt
Edward A Jones
Edward Bannister
Edward Bouchet

Edward Brooke
Edward Burghardt
Elder Lonnie
Eldridge Cleaver
Eldzier Cortor
Elijah McCoy
Elijah Muhammad
Elijah P Lovejoy
Elizabeth Taylor
Greenfield
Ellen Frances Harper
Ellen Stewart
Elliott Robert
Ellis Wade
Ellis Wilson
Ellison Ralph
Elton Wolfe
Emanuel B. Thrompson
Epheram Blackman
Eric Walrond
Ernest Wilkins
Ernie Crichlow
Erskine Tate
Esputa John
Estavanico Stephen
Ethel Waters
Etta Barnett
Etta Moten
Eubie Blake
Eugene Kinckle Jones
Eugene V McCarty
Evanti Lillian
Ferdinand Barnett
Ferdinand Jean
Ferdinand Morton
Ferrit Caesar
Ferrit John
Finley Wilson
Fletcher Henderson
Florence Mills
Fraction Carl
Francis L Cardozo
Frank L Gillespie
Frank Neal
Frank Silvera

Frank Wilsoti
Frank Wyley
Franklin Hope
Frederick Douglass
Frederick Flemister
Gall Foster
Garland Penn
Garnet Henry Highland
Garret A Morgan
Garrett James
Garrison William Lloyd
Gene Boland
George Bridgetower
George Forbes
George H White
George Haynes
George Henderson
George Liele
George Schulyer
George W .Murray
George W Lee
George W. Williams
George Walker
George Washington
Carver
Geraldine McCullough
Gerit Smith
Gloria Davy
Gloria Foster
Godfrey Cambridge
Gordon Roger Parks
Grace Bumbry
Granville Woods
Greg Morris
GreRory Ridley
Gustavus Vassa
Gwendolyn Brooks
Hale Woodruff
Hall Lloyd
Hannibal Abram
Harl Hyman
Harold E Finley
Harper T Phillips
Harriet Tubman
Harry Belafonte

Harry Burleigh
Harry Dolan
Harry H Pace
Henri Christophe
Henry Adams
Henry Cheatham
Henry Flipper
Henry Ford
Henry J. Jr Richardson
Henry McNeal Turner
Henry Ossawa Tanner
Herman E Moore
Hezekiah Grice
Hilda Simms
Himes Chester
Hiram Revels
Holmes William
Hookie Williams
Horace Cayton
Hosea Williams
Howard Thurman
Hubert M Thaxton
Hughie Lee-Smith
Ida B. Wells
Ingram Zell
Ira Aldridge
Isaac Myers
Isaiah T Montgomery
Ivan Dixon
J Standard
J. H Dickinson
J. H. ackson
J W Loguen
J. W. C Pennington
Jack Jordan
Jacob Lawrence
Jacques Clemorgan
James Augustine Healy
James B. Parsons
James Baldwin
James Beckwourth
James Birney
James Bland
James Cobb
James Derham

James Earl Jones
James Forten
James H Robinson
James Heullett
James Iewis
James Lesesne Wells
James Matthew
James McCune Smith
James Monroe Trotter
James O'Hara
James Reese
James Skip
James Weldon Johnson
Jan Ernst Matzeliger
Jean Jacques Dessalines
Jean Lalime
Jean Toomer
Jefferson Lon R
Jennings Wilmer
Jeremiah Haralson
Jesse Jackson
Jessie Redmond Fauset
Jewel Stratford
Lafontant
Jim Brown
Jimmie Mosely
Joe "King" Oliver
Joe Turner
John 0 Killen
John A Williams
John A. Hyman
John Arterberry
John B. Russwurm
John Brown
John Chavis
John E. Wideman
John H. Johnson
John H. Sengstacke
John Hope
John Hurt
John Jasper
John Jones
John Kinzie
John Mercer Langston
John Merrick

John R Lynch
John R Work
John R. Johnson
John Smythe
Johnson Hall
Jonathan C Gibbs
Jonathan Wright
Joseph Cinque
Joseph Logan
Joseph S. Sanders
Joseph T. Walls
Josephine Baker
Josh White
Juan Latino
Juanita Stout
Julian Lewis
Julian Mayfield
Julius H Taylor
Jupiter Hammon
Katherine Dunham
Kelly Miller
Langston Hughes
Lank Leonard Teon
Laura Warin Wheeling
Lawrence A Jones
Lawrence Winters
Lemuel Haynes
Leon Bibb
Leonidas Berry
LeRoi Jones
Lerone Bennett
Leslie Ferry
Lester Granger
Lewis Adams
Lewis H Latimer
Lloyd Ferguson
Loften Mitchell
Lois Mailou Jones
Lorraine Hansberry
Lott Cary
Louis Armstrong
Louis Blanchette
Louis Gossett
Louis T. Wright
Lunsford Lane

Macon B Alien
Madame C. J Walker
Mal Goode
Malcolm X.
Malvin Gray Johnson
Mansa Musa
Marcus Garvey
Margaret Butcher
Margaret Walker
Alexander
Margaret Wycherly
Marion Cook
Marion Perkins
Marjorie Lawson
Mark Miles Fisher
Marlin Smith
Martin de Porres
Martin Luther King Jr.
Martin R. Delany
Mary McIeod Bethune
Massacre Boston
Matthew A. Henson
May Howard Jackson
McDonald Leonard
McHenry Jones
Melvin B Tolson
Meredith Gourdine
Middleton H.
Lambright Jr.
Miles Davis
Montapue Cobb
Mordecai Johnson
Mother Hale
Motley Willard
Nat Turner
Nathaniel Calloway
Nathaniel Dett
Navid Walker
Nelson Mandela
Nichelle Nichols
Nnamdi Azikiwe
Nobel Sissle
Norbert Rillieux
Norman A. Simon
Oliver Cromwell

Oscar Brown
Oscar DePriest
Ossie Davis
Otis Young
Owen Dobson
Palmer Hayden
Papa Charlie Jackson
Parker Pillsbury
Paul Cuffe
Paul Laurence Dunbar
Paul R. Williams
Paul Robeson
Pauline Hopkins
Pearl Bailey
Pearl Chavers
Percy Julian
Percy RodriKues
Peter Marshall Murray
Peter Salem
Peter Williams
Phil Cohran
Philip A. Payton Jr.
Phillis Wheatley
Pierre Rodin
Pierre Toussaint
L'Ouverture
Pinckney Benton
Donald Reid
Pomp Blackman
Pomp Fisk
Prince Hall
Prince Whipple
Prudence Crandall
Queen Mother Moore
Ra Nahesi
Rafer Johnson
Ralph D. Abernathy
Raymond P. Alexander
Raymond St. Jacques
Raymond Wilkin
Richard Alien
Richard B. Harrison
Richard H. Cain
Richard H. Graves
Richard H. Hunt

Richard Wright
Richmond Barth
Ridgeley Torrence
Robert Barnes
Robert Blackburn
Robert Dean Pharr
Robert DeLarge
Robert Duncanson
Robert Goodwin
Robert Gould Shaw
Robert Hooks
Robert L. Vann
Robert Macbeth
Robert McFerrin
Robert Pious
Robert R.Church
Robert S Abbott
Robert Smalls
Roland Hayes
Romare Bearden
Rosa Parks
Roy Wilkins
Ruby Dee
Rudolph Fisher
Sadie T. Alexander
Sahala Mariem
Samuel B. Onwuchekwa
Samuel C. Taylor
Samuel J. Lee
Samuel M. Nabrit
Sarah Sedgewick
Bowers
Sargent Johnson
Scott Joplin
Selma Burke
Seymour Burr
Sinclair Drake
Singers Fisk Jubilee
Sisseretta Jones
Sojourner Truth
Solomon Humphries
Sonni All
Sonny Terry
Spencer Robinson
Stephen Myers

Stephen Smith
Sterling Brown
Sutton E. Griggs
Tack Sissons
Tames Varick
Ted Ward
Thelma Oliver
Thelonius Monk
Theodore K. Lawless
Theodore S Wright
Thomas E Miller
Thomas Fortune
Thomas Paul
Thomy Lafen
Thurgood Marshall
Timothy Wilson
Todd Duncan
Tom Dent
Toseph A Pierce
Truman K. Gibson
Ulysses Grant Dailey
Ulysses Kay
W. A. Lavalette
W. H. Jackson
Waddell Chesnutt
Waiter Francis White
Wallace Thurman
Warren E Henry
Warrick Fuller
Washington Wade
Waters Turpin
Wells Barnett
Wendell Phillips
Whitney M Young
Wilbert Warren
Wiley Jones
William A Hinton
William Attaway
William Brady
William Branch
William Carney
William Carter
William Collins
William Cooper
William Farrour

William Grant Still
William H Johnson
William H. Hastie
William Harper
William Hart
William Heard
William J. Simmons
William L. Dawson
William Leidesdorff
William Marshall
William McCurine
William Melvin Kelly
William S. Scarborough
William Still
William Warfield
William Wells Brown
William Whipper
Wole Soyinka
Zora Neal Hurston

GLOSSARY

Ade   Crown
Afo   First market day
Agha   War
Agu   Strong, Capable
Agwu   The divination diety
Akin   Valiant Warrior
Ala   land
Awo   Secret cult
Ayan   Sound of drums
Ayo   Joy
Chi   Personal god
Chuku, Chukwu   God
Eegun   Ritual mask
Efun   Guardian of the fields
Eke   Third market day
Ekun   Weeping
Idi   festival New Yam festival
Ifa   Augury, divination
Iga   Palace
Igbo   Ibo The Biafrans
Ikeji   New Yam festival
Ikenga   Warrior
Muo   Spirits, ancestors
Ndu   Life
Nkwo   Final market day
Oba   King
Ode   Hunter
Odu   Oracular utterance
Ogun   War
Oje   The living one
Oke   The hill
Ola   Fame
Olorun   Owner of Heaven
Olu   God
Oluwa   Lord the master
Omi   Water
Omo   Children
Ona   Artistic genius

Opa   Plenty
Orie   Second market day
Oruko   Abiku Infant mortality
Osin   Chief
Oso   Seer, wizard
Osun   River
Osun   Yoruba river
Oya   River Niger
Oye   Titled post
Tunde   Reincarnation

ABBREVIATIONS

F   Female
M   Male
AA   African-American
WA   Western Africa
CA   Central Africa
SA   Southern Africa
NA   Northern Africa
EA   Easthern Africa
GK   Greek
NK   Nicknames

Chinyere, Zoe aka Guggin

Tyra Mason Onwuchekwa is a former miss Caribbean, USA and author of the children books series: *Chichi Babies*™.

Dr. Sam Chekwas is the author of Ogbanje, son of the gods. He is active in the translation and introduction of African and African American history and literature in the Greek language.

Tyra and Sam are proud parents of a princess called Guggin.